A
SEASONAL
GUIDE
TO
INDOOR
GARDENING

A SEASONAL GUIDE TO INDOOR GARDENING

Jack Kramer

*Drawings
by Robert Johnson*

 LYONS & BURFORD, PUBLISHERS

Printed in the United States of America

10   9   8   7   6   5   4   3   2   1

Library of Congress Cataloging-in-Publication Data

Kramer, Jack, 1927–
    A seasonal guide to indoor gardening / Jack Kramer ; drawings by Robert Johnson.
        p.   cm.
    Originally published: Boston : Houghton Mifflin, 1976.
    Includes index.
    ISBN 1-55821-198-5
    1. Indoor gardening.   2. House plants.   I. Title.
[SB419.K726   1992]
635.9′65—dc20   92-19714
                                                               CIP

CONTENTS

INTRODUCTION HOW TO GARDEN WITH THE SEASONS

INDOOR PLANTS are as keenly attuned to the seasonal pattern of growth as outdoor ones. They require a feeding and watering schedule that fluctuates as the weather does. In fall and winter when there is little sun, for instance, plants simply cannot assimilate great quantities of food or water. Since plants have been programmed by nature for millions of years to this seasonal pattern, it makes good sense for the indoor gardener to work with nature.

In spring, plants can be readied for new growth — by repotting and trimming, for example. When plants are growing rapidly in the summer, they need more food. Ventilation is important too in very hot weather. In autumn, plants naturally slow down and their feeding and watering must be adjusted accordingly, and in winter, when many plants rest, still another set of cultural rules is needed to keep plants healthy.

This book — which of course is divided into the four seasons — includes under each season a chapter on what to do for plant families (orchids, bromeliads, gesneriads, and so on). Since each family contains a multitude of different plants (there are 25,000 orchids, 400 bromeliads, about 700 gesneriads), the what-to-do-each-season list *must be general*. However, in the seasonal plant description sections, a total of 365 specific plants are discussed, with cultural instructions. Here you will find columneas from the gesneriad family, ascocentrums from the orchid group, aspleniums from the fern family, and so on, each one described and accompanied by a drawing for identification. Even if your plant is not in these illustrated sections you can still obtain information about it from the general seasonal chapters.

Each of the four categories of plant descriptions includes those plants that I have found through the years to be generally best for that particular season. This does not mean that a plant from the spring list cannot be grown in winter or one from the summer list cannot be grown in fall. In fact, you will find that cultural instructions for *the rest of the year* are added for each plant.

This book, then, is an encyclopedia for indoor plants that you can use by itself or as a supplement to any specialized garden book. Its arrangement is deliberate: whatever the time of year, you can pick it up and find out how to grow the plants you have or want.

PART ONE

SPRING

1 PREPARING PLANTS FOR SPRING

JUST WHEN you think winter may never end, your indoor plants start sending signals that spring is almost here. Although it may be snowy and very cold outside, the leaves are perking up on your plants and fresh new shoots are sprouting from their stems. The cycle of nature is already at work. When I lived in Chicago, my house plants were my guideline to the weather. Even in February when I looked at my window plants I could see that spring was well on its way.

February and March are the months for refreshing the indoor garden; good weather is on the way, and plants are ready to make lush growth. But first they need some pruning and trimming and after that repotting with new soil with adequate nutrients. Many plants — most palms and ferns, for example — produce new growth only in spring and summer, so it's essential that they have material to grow on.

SOIL MIXES

Outdoors, plant roots can stretch and strive and find fresh soil and nutrients. But indoor plants are confined to the containers we put them in. Since they can't look for food on their own, it is up to us to bring them the fresh soil necessary for a new season of growth. Spring is a good time to learn about soil mixes.

1

Years ago, local nurseries sold bulk soil — mealy, humusy black loam that smelled of the earth, a complete soil with all necessary nutrients. Today, bulk soil is rarely available except in large quantities, too much for the average indoor gardener and out of the question for the apartment dweller.

The solution is to buy packaged soil, for both speed and convenience. The problem with packaged soils is that there are so many trade names and different soil mixes it is difficult to sort the good from the bad. There are soils for African violets, for cacti, for geraniums, so-called house plant soil, soil for gesneriads. You can never determine exactly what is inside the packages — just what is the minuscule difference that separates the soil for geraniums from soil for African violets? Even if the contents were listed on the package (and they aren't), it would still take a soil expert to determine which is the best mixture. I suggest you buy a standard house plant mix. You can add ingredients to it for different kinds of plants, as explained later.

To test packaged soil, squeeze the bag; it should be pliable and soft to the touch. A good soil has porosity — air spaces between the soil

A group of African violets and ferns bring spring to this window long before outside trees and shrubs start their display. (Photo by Matthew Barr)

Good soil is mealy and porous; it has a grainy feel to it and is never dry or sandy. (Photo USDA)

particles — and is neither clayey to the touch nor sandy. Unfortunately, you can't smell the soil in the package; good soil has an earthy or humusy smell, so look for rich black soil and avoid the package that looks old or caked or light gray. Chances are that the soil no longer has adequate nutrient content.

In addition to the house plant soil, buy a small bag of compost or humus.

When you get home, add 2 cups of humus to 1 cubic foot (a standard large sack) of house plant soil. Mix the materials thoroughly; use a bucket and a wooden stick, or your hands.

I use this mixture for all my plants, with the following exceptions:

For flowering plants, I add 2 tablespoons of bone meal.

For cacti and succulents, I substitute 1 cup of sand for the compost.

For orchids, I used packaged fir bark.

If you don't use all the soil at one time, store the remainder in a tightly covered canister or plastic bag in a cool place so that it doesn't dry out and get flaky.

Some people are perfectionists; they take the time to mix their own soil from basic ingredients. I heartily recommend this if you can, because when you mix your own soil, you control what goes into it from the start. The standard recipe for mix-your-own soil is 1 part garden loam, 1 part sand, and 1 part leaf mold.

Just what is garden loam? Is it soil from outdoors? Soil you buy? Soil you mix? When I called the Department of Agriculture to ask

This plectranthus has become spindly and out of proportion; it is being trimmed back with a pocketknife. The minor surgery will encourage new bushy growth and cutting does not harm the plant. (Photo by Matthew Barr)

them what garden loam was, I got several different answers. Through the years I have developed my own definition of garden loam, which I think is simple and worth passing on. Garden loam is soil that has some clay, leaf mold, and sand in it. It is similar to well-cultivated soil you find in flower beds.

The sand you want for your soil mix is called "sharp sand" or "builders' sand." Avoid salty seashore sand or very fine powdery sand, and be sure what you use is free from salt or debris.

Leaf mold is decayed or rotted leaves or other organic matter — the material you get from a compost pile.

Here, then, is the soil recipe in easy form:

    1 part garden loam (or packaged soil)

    1 part clean sand

    1 part leaf mold or compost

    1 tablespoon perlite (or small stones) to ensure that the soil is porous and has air spaces.

Most orchids and bromeliads need an entirely different potting mixture. Redwood bark chips is the best medium for 90 percent of all orchids and comes in several different grades. Medium grade is usually used and is easy to work with, and is now the accepted growing medium for orchids. Bark is available in so-called hobby sacks. (The ladyslipper and cymbidium orchids require equal parts of ground bark and soil.) Redwood or fir bark comes in three

After the cut is made, burn a match, extinguish it, and then rub the charcoal over the open wound to seal the cut. This will eliminate any possible disease organisms entering stem. (Photo by Matthew Barr)

grades: small, medium, and large (⅛, ¼, and ½ inch in diameter); most orchids do fine in medium bark.

CONTAINERS AND SAUCERS

We'll discuss ornamental containers in Chapter 8. Here we'll consider the most popular house plant containers: the terra cotta clay pot and the glazed clay pot. The terra cotta pot is *the* best housing for plants because moisture evaporates easily from its walls and the soil remains at an even temperature.

The design of terra cotta pots has gone far beyond the standard, but still most useful, pot we all know. The last time I was at the nursery I counted seventeen different styles in fourteen different sizes. Among them were Italian pots, Spanish pots, Venetian pots, azalea pots, bowl pots, dish pots, bulb pans, planter boxes, square pots, strawberry jars, and pots shaped like chickens.

With so many container styles available, you can select the one that suits your plant's appearance and growth habits. Round bushy plants look good in bowl or dish pots; tall vertical plants are striking in cylinders. Graceful flamboyant plants like ferns are dramatic in Spanish pots. If your plants have deep roots, use the deepest container. If plants have scant, short roots, use the shortest pot; too much unused soil tends to get soggy and rot the roots. Soak any new clay pot a few hours so it will absorb water, or the pot will take away moisture from the soil when you plant.

Glazed pottery containers used to be more handsome than healthy for plants. But manufacturers have finally started putting drainage holes in these pots, so do try them. Glazed pots come in colors; many people like to coordinate the color with room furnishings. Pots have shiny or matte finishes, and the basic shape is like that of the standard terra cotta pot. Remember that moisture can't evaporate through the glazed walls as it does in terra cotta, so the soil holds moisture longer. The shiny glazed pots are also prone to chipping.

There are hundreds of plastic pots for plants; some are flexible and others are rigid plastic. Like the glazed pots, plastic ones hold moisture longer than clay. I don't recommend small plastic pots because tall or heavy plants tend to topple over in them. Yet you may like the colors and the clean look of some of these pots. Plastic acrylic ones are clear, almost glass-like. They're elegant in appearance and heavier than normal plastic. Most acrylic pots are ⅛ to ¼ inch thick. I use these pots where I want a special effect (roots and soil are visible).

If you're growing plants in pots on windowsills or tables, the wood must be protected from water stain. Buy a saucer at the time you buy the pot or you'll have to hunt and search later for a particular size. If you use an unglazed terra cotta saucer, moisture will seep through, so put a cork mat or attractive hot plate protector under the saucer to eliminate this problem. This is especially important if you put plants on fine furniture.

HOW TO POT PLANTS

Plants in pots up to 10 inches in diameter need repotting annually. Plants in larger pots should be repotted every two years. Take a lesson from Mother Nature; when you see new buds and tiny leaves started outdoors, your indoor plants too are ready to grow!

Plants confined to small pots use up the soil's nutrients in a period of six to ten months, so you must repot yearly if you want to keep plants with you throughout all the seasons. Many people think that if they feed plants heavily to furnish nutrients they don't need to supply fresh soil. But excessive feeding actually locks in nutrients, and causes toxic salts to build up, which harms plants — overfeeding has caused the demise of many house plants. Repotting is the most important part of good plant culture, so let's consider the right way to do it and then discuss how to care for plants after they are repotted, to help them adjust to the transplanting.

Most plants need plenty of water. What they do *not* need — and can't survive — is standing water, so you should start with a pot with a drainage hole. But just the hole is not enough; you also need drainage materials to provide a filtering system at the bottom of the pot. This system will help distribute water and ensure that no excess water gathers at the bottom of the pot to cause a harmful stagnant soil. Soil without drainage materials can become packed and waterlogged, even with the most careful watering procedures. To eliminate this problem, put some gravel at the bottom of the pot before you fill it with soil. Generally, I use ½ to 1 inch of gravel (but *not* pea-sized smooth stones) to a container. If you don't have gravel, use small broken pot pieces of about ½ inch diameter, small stones, or any type of clay material with uneven surfaces so water can be distributed over many areas to evaporate readily.

Charcoal chips aren't specifically drainage materials, but they help keep soil sweet. Charcoal chips are available in small boxes or bags. Just sprinkle 1 tablespoon of chips into the bottom of a 6 to 10-inch pot, or 2 tablespoons for larger pots, on top of the gravel or stones.

Whether you are *potting* up a new plant, or *repotting* an old one into a larger container, the procedure is basically the same. Before you can repot, though, you must remove the plant from the pot it is in. It is best to repot a plant when the soil is slightly dry, rather than wet.

To remove the plant from its container, hold the pot upright and tap the edge of the container against the edge of a worktable. Do this several times, but try not to crack the pot. This procedure loosens the soil ball enough so you can remove the plant without harming the root systems. Now grasp the collar of the plant with one hand, hold the pot with the other hand, and gently tease the plant from the pot.

The cissus vine has become too large for its indoor place and is being cut back and groomed. Such cutting will produce new growth at the base and help provide greenery where it is needed to produce a bushier plant. (Photo by Matthew Barr)

This spider plant is ready for repotting; note the network of crowded roots. Fresh soil is badly needed so the plant can keep growing. (Photo by Matthew Barr)

If the plant doesn't come out of the pot, don't pull hard or you'll tear the roots. Instead, take a hammer and gently tap the outside of the pot, to crack it. This means you will lose the old pot, but it's better to save the plant than the pot. When you've removed the plant (with root ball intact), crumble away some of the old soil — not too much — and trim away any dead roots.

Be sure your new pot is thoroughly clean. If it is a new clay pot, remember to soak it in water for a few hours so it won't absorb water the plants need. Cover the drainage hole with a small square of hardware cloth (screen) and put the gravel over that. Now pour a mound of soil on top of the gravel. Next, center the plant so the collar of the plant is above the rim of the pot. If the plant is too high, take out some soil; if the plant is too low, add soil to the mound. Fill in and around the plant with soil to ½ inch of the top of the pot. Firm the soil in place with your thumbs; press down, but not with undue pressure. (You want to eliminate air pockets but not compact the soil.) After you do this you'll notice that still more soil is needed to reach the ½-inch mark. Add the additional soil, tap the bottom of the pot on the table again, firm the soil with your thumbs, and water the plant thoroughly. Wait a few minutes and then soak the soil again.

Repotting a plant is minor surgery, so your plant needs a little help to get going again. Don't immediately put a repotted plant in a sunny place, because the roots aren't ready yet to work to full capacity. A bright but not sunny place is the best location. Water the plant moderately; try to keep the soil evenly moist. Watch the plant daily for about a week to see how it's reacting.

If plants are having trouble in recovering from repotting, use a plastic Baggie or Saran Wrap cover (as explained in Chapter 2) to ensure good humidity, which helps contribute to healthy new growth. Once new growth shows, the plant can be moved to its permanent place.

PLANT FOODS AND FEEDING

The plant food manufacturers have gone wild in recent years, flooding the market with many different kinds of plant foods. Feeding plants has become almost as difficult for some people as selecting the right formula for a baby. But don't let the food hassle hassle you. Basically, plants just need nitrogen, phosphorus, and potash. Nitrogen makes plants grow leaves, phosphorus makes plants grow healthy stems, and potash helps plants resist diseases. There are other benefits from each element, but essentially that's the picture. Every plant food you buy has the contents of nitrogen, phosphorus, and potash marked on the bottle or package. Some say 10-10-5, others 20-20-10, and so on. In each case, the percentage of nitrogen is denoted by the first figure, phosphorus by the second, and potash by the

Here old soil is being crumbled away (gently) from the roots so they have a chance to grow. (Photo by Matthew Barr)

third. Most plant foods have other trace elements necessary for plant growth. There are at least a dozen different formulas available, but a basic 10-10-5 plant food — which is neither too weak nor too strong — administered at proper times is all you'll need for most plants.

Besides the different formulas offered, plant foods come in several forms: soluble (powders to be mixed with water), granular (pellets to be sprinkled on soil, then watered), tablets (to be dissolved in water), liquid plant foods (to be mixed with water), and time-released plant foods (in capsule form). Of all the plant foods, granular is the most convenient to use; all you do is sprinkle the granules on the soil and water it. Powders can be messy in the home, tablets sometimes do not disintegrate or spread well, and the time-released capsules (which supply food for several months) are chancy because too much food over too long a time beyond your control may do the plants more harm than good.

There are also plant foods specifically made for African violets, philodendrons, cacti, and so on. I have found little value in specialized plant foods and I just use a basic plant food, such as 10-10-5, to keep my plants growing well. This food comes in easy-to-apply granular form.

In addition to these man-made plant foods, there are natural helpers. Natural plant foods may be harder to find but they are often better than the commercial fertilizers. These organic foods include cottonseed meal, fish emulsion, bone meal, bloodmeal, and dry steer and cow manure. All are excellent sources of nitrogen; some are now in tidy packages at nurseries.

Specific directions for feeding are in the seasonal check lists and plant descriptions. Here are some general rules to follow:

1. Never feed an ailing plant, because it can't absorb the food.
2. Never try to force a plant into growth with excessive feeding or you'll kill the plant.
3. Be sure soil is moist before you feed plants.
4. Never feed seedlings; it takes a while before they can absorb food.

WATERING

Specific instructions for watering are in plant descriptions and seasonal check lists but here are some general hints on watering plants.

Do you worry that your water supply contains too much chlorine or trace elements that may injure plants? Well, if you can drink the water, your plants can drink it too without ill effects. The temperature of the water is probably more important than the quality of the water. Very cold water shocks plants; the warm roots get a sudden chilling from cold water and can't absorb the moisture as they should. Tepid water is best for plants.

The new pot for the spider plant is shown with drainage material (pieces of clay pots) being placed inside. (Photo by Matthew Barr)

Many people insist that you should water plants only in the morning. But I've watered plants at midday and at night without harming them. The morning-watering rule may be true for outdoor gardens, but indoors, it's of little importance.

When you water plants, really water them; scanty watering creates dry pockets in the soil, and when roots reach the dry area, they stop growing. How do you know when you have watered a plant sufficiently? Watch to see that excess water drains into the saucer; throw it away and then water the plant again. Once more remove the excess water. If the soil is porous and fertile and all other conditions good, this type of watering makes plants thrive.

Large pots hold water longer than small ones. Clay pots lose moisture faster than plastic or glazed ones. Some plants soak up water at a faster rate than others, and some plants prefer different amounts of moisture at the roots. Ferns like it very moist, for example, while dieffenbachias do not. Thus, in plant descriptions I have advised: "Keep soil evenly moist" or "Dry out between waterings." This way you need not be concerned too much about pot size or type of pot. To determine if the soil is dry or evenly moist, test it with your finger; push down slightly into the soil. If the soil feels somewhat dry — doesn't give to the touch — it's time to water. If the soil gives under pressure from the finger, don't water. It's much better to err on the dry side than to continually sop plants.

A milk bottle or a cup is no substitute for a watering can; both the metal and plastic type are fine. Buy a watering container with a long spout so you can easily reach plant soil. A container with a "rose" (a shower head) on the end of the spout is even better because the rose releases a gentle flow of water rather than a gushing stream to knock out soil.

Water your plants slowly and carefully, making sure the water gets into the soil, not just on the foliage or in the saucer. If you have the time and patience, take your plants to the sink and water them there. Some people put all their plants in the bathtub and turn on the shower, which is really a very good way to water many plants — if they aren't too heavy. Overhead watering is good for plants because it wets not only the soil but also the foliage. (Most plants like water on the leaves; the exceptions are the hairy-leaved African violets and other gesneriads.)

Once a month take each and every one of your plants to the sink, fill the sink with water, and set the pots in the water. When air bubbles stop appearing on the surface of the soil, take the pot out and let the excess water drain off.

On top of the pieces of pot, soil is put in place; use a mound of soil and then center plant. (Photo by Matthew Barr)

TRIMMING AND GROOMING

No matter how well you feed and water them, plants will have straggly leaves and ill-shaped growth unless you trim, groom, and train them into shape. Unfortunately, most people can't bear to snip off a leaf or cut away a healthy stem or branch. When some of my visitors see me hacking away at a plant, they react as if they were witnessing a horror movie. But removing leaves and cutting off old branches encourages fresh growth, gets rid of decayed areas that can attract fungus infection, and generally adds to the health of the plant. What I advocate is not radical surgery, just some cosmetic help.

Recognize the growth habits of the plants. Some are rosette in shape, others are more pyramidal, still others are branching. Don't hack away without reason. Trim the plant as nature would want it, conforming to the growth habit. Since it's difficult to do this at close range where the eye can't discern the overall shape, look at the plant from a distance before you take shears in hand.

Use a small pruning scissors (a bonsai type is good) or shears, and have a pocketknife at hand. After you cut a plant, be sure to sterilize

Tamp soil into place around the collar of the plant. Soil should be firm and compact so there are no air holes. (Photo by Matthew Barr)

the scissors and knife in case the plant harbored a hidden disease. Sterilize by running a flame over the metal. Use the scissors or shears to remove leaves and stems; use the knife to cut small branches and woody growth. Always cut an an angle. Seal open wounds with charcoal from a burnt match so there aren't any open cells for fungus to attack. After the spring trimming, let the plant rest and keep the soil barely moist for a few weeks; then resume routine watering.

Grooming is something different from trimming; it's picking off dead leaves and blossoms to keep the top of the soil free of debris. If you see a yellow leaf or a decayed blossom, get rid of it quickly, because it's an invitation to pesty critters. Grooming also includes keeping the container clean. Dirt, scum, or algae on the container is unsightly and can attract insects.

Spring is the best time to trim plants; in winter your paring may start plants into growth too soon, before the biological clock within them is ready to respond to growing. Mother Nature does the job outdoors with great storms that snap off tree branches and strip leaves from plants. But indoors you must be Mother Nature. Time it naturally and all will be well.

2 GROW YOUR OWN

THERE'S a lot of fun in starting plants from seed, watching small specks growing into healthy young plants. And think of the money you save! If you have never tried growing house plants from seed, here's an interesting new project for spring. Check the list at the end of this chapter for suitable varieties.

SOWING SEED

You can grow seeds in terra cotta pots, but since a package contains many seeds, you really should use somewhat larger containers: shallow wooden fruit boxes and plastic storage boxes, about 10 inches wide by 14 inches long by 8 inches deep, are good propagation containers. So are egg cartons (put seed in each cup), frozen roll trays, or almost any other container about 4 to 5 inches deep. Just make sure you put small drainage holes at the bottom of any container so excess water can escape. Heat the end of an ice pick to make holes in rigid plastic containers.

You can also sow seeds in peat pots. Fill these with soil, insert a seed, and when the leaves are up, transplant, pot and all. This saves some of the shock of moving the plants to fresh soil. Seed pellets or discs are also available; with these, insert seed and water. No other growing medium is needed; the pellet expands and becomes the container. When leaves are up, the expanded pellet is planted in soil.

Generally, I use a terra cotta pot to start seeds because it is cheap and handy. I am not concerned if only half the seeds germinate. I don't want acres of plants; only enough for my indoor gardens and greenhouse.

Years ago seed was started in soil — any old soil — but often the soil wasn't sterile and contained fungus that caused young plants to develop a disease called "damping-off" and die young. So seed-starting materials that were sterile and porous were introduced. Today these "starters" include a number of products, but vermiculite seems to be the most popular. Perlite, sand, sphagnum moss, and sterile soil also are good starters.

There's always a great deal of unnecessary discussion about how deep to plant seeds. Imbed the seed about ¼ inch into the starting medium if the seed is large, say $\frac{1}{16}$ or ⅛ inch. If the seed is small, specklike, sprinkle it on top of the medium and then add a thin layer of sterile soil over the seed.

Seed can be started in a standard clay pot like this or in any 3 to 5-inch household container that has drainage holes. (Photo by Matthew Barr)

Started in a plastic cottage-cheese carton, these seeds have sprouted and in a few more days will be ready for transplanting into separate containers. (Photo by Jack Barnick)

Seed can also be started in peat pots like this. When it is time to transplant, the complete pot is put into soil; this eliminates some of the shock of the transplanting. (Photo by Matthew Barr)

To start, fill the bottom of your container (about ½ inch) with small stones or pieces of broken clay pots. Add the growing medium, and then moisten it a bit. (I usually spray the medium gently with water several times until all moisture is soaked up.) Now, depending on the size of the seed, scatter seed on top of the medium or imbed the seed. Again spray the starter very gently, and place the container in a warm (72 to 78°F) shaded place. This whole easy process shouldn't take more than fifteen minutes — sowing seed *is* simple.

Put a layer of Saran Wrap or a Baggie propped on four sticks over the seed tray or box or pot. This creates a tiny greenhouse that will provide adequate humidity to keep the growing medium moist, the essential part of germination. The medium *must* be uniformly moist; even one drying out may be fatal. On the other hand, too much moisture can cause damping-off disease, so check the medium daily; if too much moisture appears on the inside of the plastic, remove it for a few hours.

Seeds of most house plants need warmth to germinate. Ideally, warmth should come from underneath the container. Put the container on top of a refrigerator (temperatures there are usually 72°F or more). Don't use the tops of radiators because this heat is fluctuating and liable to be either too intense or too low. You can also use low-voltage heating cables, which supply a constant heat of 70 to 78°F. Some containers come with cables.

Germination time is from several days to several months; it all depends on the plant and cultural conditions. To be on the safe side, never throw seeds away before six months have elapsed. When the

Cuttings taken from mature plants can be rooted in plastic bags of vermiculite. The bag is tied to ensure that humidity gathers inside to furnish moisture for cuttings and make rooting easier. (Photo by USDA)

first tiny green shoots appear, give seedlings more air; that is, remove the plastic most of the day. When the first true leaves sprout, the plastic can be discarded. Just remember that during the entire germination time the medium must be kept uniformly moist, never wet.

Many times you'll have more seedlings than you want. This is nothing to fret about; there are always friends to give them to. Once the seedlings have their second pair of leaves, thin them out so the stronger plants have space to grow; that is, discard the weaker plants. You can remove the excess plants with tweezers, or gently pick them out of the starting medium with a pencil. Leave the other plants in the container a few more days or until they are large enough to handle. Then remove the plants from the container and put each plant in a separate, 2-inch pot. Do this gently so the root ball is disturbed as little as possible. (This is why peat pots and cubes come in handy: they can be lifted out almost intact.)

Now be sure to put the pot in a terrarium or moisture-proof enclosed area for several days so plants get over the shock of transplanting. Again, use a Baggie or Saran Wrap to protect plants from fluctuating temperatures and drying out. And be sure the soil doesn't get too moist during this transplant time. Use a sterile packaged house plant soil for transplants.

When the new seedlings are a few inches high, repot them into permanent containers. Don't put plants in very large pots because too much unused soil can become too dry or wet. Generally, a 3 or 4-inch pot suits seedlings very well. Use a packaged porous soil and repot as outlined in Chapter 1.

CUTTINGS, DIVISION

Sowing seed to get new plants is easy, although it does take some time and experience to get *everything* to grow. But taking cuttings of plants or dividing them to get new plants requires only a few minutes. If you want more plants of some particular species you already have, it is a simple matter to snip a cutting or to divide a mature plant to get two plants.

Some cuttings — tradescantia or philodendron — need only be placed in water; wait for roots to form, then plant the cutting. But most need to be rooted in a growing medium. A cutting consists of 3 or 4 inches from the top of a plant stem. The best time to start cuttings is in spring; this is the natural time of growing. You can use any kind of container — the same ones you used for seeds — and the same growing medium. Put 3 or 4 inches of vermiculite or perlite in the bottom of the container. Dip the cut stem end in a rooting hormone and insert the cutting about 2 inches into the medium. Because most cuttings need good humidity to form roots, place a Baggie over the container in a tent fashion (on sticks) to trap humidity.

Getting two plants from a large one by division is a simple operation. Note that this Chinese evergreen has several crowns so a division is possible. (Photo by Matthew Barr)

The large plant has been unpotted and this photo shows the two crowns or divisions ready for separate pots. (Photo by Matthew Barr)

Here is a single division in a smaller pot ready for growing-on in spring. (Photo by Matthew Barr)

Keep the growing medium evenly moist, neither dry nor soggy, and place the cuttings in a warm (75°F) location in a shady place. In a few weeks remove the plastic tent. Tug the cutting gently to see if it has roots. If it does, transfer the new plant to a 3-inch pot of soil. If roots haven't formed, leave the cutting and wait.

You can also get new plants from leaf cuttings. Take a leaf with a portion of a stem from a mature plant. Insert the leaf upright into a container of vermiculite and put a Baggie over it or invert a glass jar over the container. Place the cutting in a shady place for a few weeks. You can also put leaf cuttings horizontally in a container of vermiculite to get new plants. To do this, first cut across the leaf veins in several places on the underside. Put the leaves right side up, flat on the sand in the container. Plantlets soon appear along the cut and draw nourishment from the mother leaf. When the new plants can be handled easily, cut them from the parent leaf and pot separately in soil. Rex begonias, kalanchoes, and African violets can all be propagated from leaves.

Division is simply pulling apart a large plant or splitting the plant with a sterile knife. By putting the plant on a low table and looking down at it, you can almost see where a natural division takes place in a plant like Chinese evergreen or a fern. The junctures are the places to perform the surgery. Put each plant in a pot of soil and allow to grow-on naturally.

You can start some plants from leaf cuttings; here an African violet is started in vermiculite. The inverted glass pot is used to keep moisture inside the "growth" chamber. (Photo by Matthew Barr)

AIR LAYERING

Plants with woody stems such as rubber trees, philodendrons, and dieffenbachias are best propagated by air layering. Either remove a strip of bark about 1 inch long directly below a leaf node or cut a V-shaped notch in the stem. In either case, wrap a big chunk of moist sphagnum moss around the bare wood and then cover it with a piece of flexible plastic secured at top and bottom with string. There must be a moisture-proof seal for growth to start.

Be patient with air layering; it may be six to nine months before roots form. You will see the roots in the moss ball; then it is time to sever the new plant just below the ball of roots and pot it.

The following chart will help you to propagate plants.

HOUSE PLANT PROPAGATION CHART

Botanical and common name	Vegetative methods	Seeds	Hints
Abutilon hybridum (flowering maple)	Cuttings	*	Needs ample humidity
Acalypha hispida (chenille plant)	Cuttings		Needs good humidity
Achimenes	Tubers	*	Requires plenty of heat
Adiantum tenerum (maidenhair fern)	Division		Easy with division
Aeschynanthus speciosus (lipstick vine)	Cuttings; air layering		Subject to damping-off fungus
Agave victoriae reginae (century plant)	Offshoots		More plants than you will need
Aglaonema commutatum (Chinese evergreen)	Cuttings; air layering	*	Cuttings easier to do than layering
Alternanthera versicolor	Cuttings; division		Difficult to start
Aphelandra chamaissiona (zebra plant)	Cuttings		Plants get leggy so take cuttings yearly
Araucaria excelsa (Norfolk Island pine)	Stem cuttings; air layering	*	Layering works well, but allow roots to form

Botanical and common name	Vegetative methods	Seeds	Hints
Asparagus sprengeri (emerald fern)	Division	*	Simple with division
Aspidistra elatior (cast-iron plant)	Division		Another easy one
Asplenium nidus (birds' nest fern)	Division		Easy
Begonia	Leaf cuttings	*	Most cuttings need ample humidity
Beloperone guttata (shrimp plant)	Tip cuttings		Not always successful
Caladium	Tubers		Start each year
Calathea concinna	Division		Watch for damping-off
Caryota mitis (fishtail palm)	Offsets; division		Slow but sure with either method
Ceropegia woodii (rosary vine)	Cuttings		Difficult
Chlorophytum elatum (spider plant)	Division or runners		Put runners in water; simple
Cissus antarctica (kangaroo vine)	Cuttings		Easy
Codiaeum (croton)	Cuttings	*	Need heat
Coffea arabica (Arabian coffee)	Cuttings		Somewhat difficult
Coleus (painted-leaf plant)	Tip cuttings	*	Needs ample humidity
Columnea	Tip cuttings		Not always successful
Davallia (rabbit's foot fern)	Division of rhizomes		Easy
Dieffenbachia (dumbcane)	Cuttings; air layering		Air layering best
Dizygotheca elegantissima (false aralia)	Cuttings; air layering		Difficult to start
Epiphyllum (orchid cactus)	Cuttings		Subject to damping-off

Botanical and common name	Vegetative methods	Seeds	Hints
Episcia	Cuttings; division		Needs ample humidity
Euphorbia pulcherrima (poinsettia)	Cuttings		Difficult
E. splendens (crown-of-thorns)	Cuttings		Easy
Ficus (figs or rubber plant)	Leaf cuttings; air layering		Air layering generally successful
Gynura aurantiaca (purple velvet plant)	Cuttings		Temperamental
Hedera (English ivy)	Cuttings	*	Easy with plenty of moisture
Hibiscus rosa-sinensis (rose-of-China)	Cuttings	*	Needs warmth and ample humidity
Hoya carnosa (wax plant)	Cuttings		Difficult but not impossible
Jacobinia carnea (king's crown)	Tip cuttings	*	Easy
Kohleria	Tip cuttings; division of rhizomes		Needs good humidity
Maranta (prayer plant)	Division; leaf-stalk cuttings		Subject to damping-off
Medinilla magnifica (love plant)	Cuttings		Difficult
Monstera deliciosa (Swiss cheese plant)	Cuttings; air layering		Air layering generally successful
Nephrolepis bostoniense (Boston fern)	Runners; division		Division easiest method
Pandanus veitchii (screw pine)	Offsets; division		Either method very simple
Pelargonium (geranium)	Cuttings		Dust ends of cutting with hormone powder
Pellaea rotundifolia (button fern)	Division		Easy in protected container

Botanical and common name	Vegetative methods	Seeds	Hints
Peperomia	Stem or leaf cuttings		Easy
Philodendron	Cuttings		For most types just place in water
Pilea (aluminum plant)	Cuttings		Cuttings usually successful
Polypodium polycarpon (polypody)	Division		Easy
Rebutia (crown cactus)		*	Seed germinates easily under lights
Rechsteineria leucotricha (Brazilian edelweiss)	Cuttings; tubers	*	Dividing tubers easiest method
Rhodea japonica	Cuttings		Will root in water
Saintpaulia (African violet)	Leaf cuttings; division	*	Simple
Sansevieria trifasciata (snake plant)	Division; cuttings		Easy with division
Saxifraga sarmentosa (strawberry geranium)	Runners		Place in water to root
Schefflera actinophylla (umbrella tree)	Cuttings; half-ripened stems	*	Somewhat difficult
Scindapsus (pothos)	Cuttings		Very easy
Smithiantha cinnabarina (temple bells)	Offshoots; stolons		Simple
Streptocarpus rexii (Cape primrose)	Cuttings; division	*	Very easy
Syngonium (arrowhead plant)	Cuttings		Grows like a weed
Vallota speciosa (Scarborough lily)	Offsets		Pot offsets when they have two pairs of leaves
Veltheimia viridifolia	Division of bulbs		Repot every year
Zebrina pendula (wandering Jew)	Root cuttings		Will root in water

3 WHAT TO DO IN SPRING

BEGONIAS

Here is a vast group of plants. Rhizomatous begonias include plants such as the beefsteak begonia (*Begonia erythrophylla*), angel-wings such as 'Pink Rubra,' and hairy-leaved begonias: *B. metallica* and *B.* 'Woolly Bear.' There are also fibrous begonias and the popular tapestry-leaved rex begonias. (Wax begonias and tuberous begonias are best grown outdoors.)

Water and Light: Rhizomatous and hairy-leaved species need good soaking this time of the year; allow the soil to dry out between waterings. The angel-wings, fibrous, and rex begonias require an evenly moist soil all season. Bright light is essential for begonias except for the rexes, which like a shady place.

Temperature and Humidity: In spring most begonias do fine with average home temperatures and humidity of 20 to 30 percent. Avoid misting plants. The hairy-leaved and rex types develop spotted foliage if water stands on the leaves and rhizomatous types can rot from too much water on stems.

Feeding: Begonias are greedy feeders and even freshly potted plants need some plant food at this time of year. Use 10-10-5 every third watering during the warm months.

Note: Repot in fresh soil yearly; these plants quickly use up nutrients in the soil.

BROMELIADS

The bromeliads as a group are perhaps the easiest of all plants to grow indoors; most have their own water reservoir in case you forget to water them, and practically all of them can survive dimly lit corners if necessary. Pot plants in equal parts fir bark and soil.

Water and Light: Keep plants somewhat dry at the roots but keep the water cups formed by the vaselike growth of the plants filled. If it has been an unusually dark winter, don't plunge bromeliads into sunlight abruptly; bright light without sun suits them best now. (In summer they can be in sun.)

Temperature and Humidity: Bromeliads grow best in warm temperatures (80°F) but they also adapt to the average home temperature of about 70°F. At this time of the year be sure bromeliads have ample ventilation. Keep a window open somewhere in the growing area or have a small fan going at low speed to keep air buoyant. The average indoor humidity of 20 to 30 percent is fine for bromeliads. Spring rains add to humidity if you keep windows open slightly.

Feeding: Most bromeliads react unfavorably to feeding, so it is best to allow plants to grow on their own as long as they have fresh potting mix. However, if you have neglected to repot bromeliads annually, then feed plants using a 10-10-5 fertilizer once a month.

BULBS

Plants growing from a bulb, tuber, or corm offer some of the finest indoor flowers. The bulbs that bloom only for a season, such as crocus and narcissus, are well known. But there are also bulbous plants such as eucharis, vallota, and veltheimia that bloom year after year.

Water and Light: Some bulbs are blooming now; some may be starting to grow. Treat the bulbs coming into bloom with even moisture and bright light. Those bulbs starting growth require scant moisture and a shady place.

Temperature and Humidity: Bulbs need cool temperatures and this isn't always possible in the home. Still, there are places indoors such as a pantry window or a room without artificial heat where plants can be placed. An ideal temperature for mature bulbs is about 60°F.

Feeding: Do not feed bulbs; the bulb itself contains nutrients necessary to support the plant.

Note: Most bulbs are started in fall and winter, and because there are so many types, culture varies. You will find how to grow them in the plant descriptions.

CACTI

Many cacti bloom indoors with large handsome flowers that dazzle the eye. Rebutias and mammillarias, echinocacti and others furnish much beauty for the home.

Water and Light: In spring most cacti are showing new growth, and at this time plants require a soil that is evenly moist, neither soggy nor dry. Be sure plants are in sun; they need it to bear flowers. Place them in east or south windows.

Temperature and Humidity: Cacti tolerate a wide range of temperatures from 65 to 90°F, but ideally should be grown at 78°F with less heat at night. Average home humidity of 20 to 30 percent is fine.

Feeding: Avoid feeding cacti; if they are in fresh soil, they will have adequate nutrients.

Note: Cacti do not grow in sand as most people believe; this may be true in the desert but not in the home. Provide a soil mix of ⅔ soil and ⅓ sand. Use a standard packaged house plant soil and add sand.

FERNS

People love ferns and people kill them at an alarming rate. Quite frankly, ferns are not easy to grow; even experienced gardeners have trouble with them. To help you keep ferns as long-time residents let me stress the importance of a good porous soil. More than most other plants, ferns require a special growing mix; I have successfully used equal parts of ground fir bark and soil for them. A soggy or packed soil will kill them.

Water and Light: In spring, ferns are starting growth and if possible should be put in fresh soil. Keep the plants evenly moist and in a bright place. Sunlight can do considerable damage. In their natural setting, ferns like shady moist locations.

Temperature and Humidity: As warm weather starts, mist plants and keep a buoyant atmosphere; moisture and coolness are important. A temperature of 65 to 70°F is fine.

Feeding: Try to avoid feeding ferns; they react adversely to plant foods. A little fish emulsion, however, at this time of year is helpful. Use it once a month.

Note: Ferns with their rosette growth tend to become crowded with fronds on top of fronds and many times lose their symmetry. It will not harm plants if you prune some fronds so that all leaves have ample breathing space. Turn plants every month or so to be sure all parts of the plant get enough light.

FLOWERING PLANTS

These are the plants that are the color bearers of the seasons. They include clerodendron, bougainvillea, ixora, hibiscus, and others (see plant descriptions).

Water and Light: Keep soil quite moist during this season; it should always be cool to the touch. Move flowering plants to windows where light is very good. Keep them in sun for flowers.

Temperature and Humidity: As the warm months start, flowering plants need more warmth. Ideal temperature for most is 75 to 80°F; of course at night a slight drop in temperature is fine. Keep humidity at a good level, 30 percent. Mist plants occasionally.

Feeding: Feed flowering plants but remember that any plant food with excessive nitrogen (first figure on plant food packages) will stimulate foliage production and deter flower production. Use a mild solution of 10-10-5 every third watering. When potting, add some bone meal to each pot of soil, one tablespoon for a 5-inch pot is fine.

FOLIAGE PLANTS

This large group of plants includes dieffenbachia, dracaena, cissus, philodendron, ficus, plectranthus, and others, and in general most can be grown in the same manner. Where exceptions occur, they are noted in plant descriptions.

Water and Light: During the spring keep foliage plants evenly moist; this is the time of year when plants can take a good amount of moisture since the weather is warmer and the light more intense. Provide good bright light for foliage plants — none really likes darkness although few want direct sun.

Temperature and Humidity: Average home temperatures are fine. To assure good growth, mist plants to help add moisture to the air, or set pots on moist beds of gravel.

Feeding: A monthly feeding program can be started now, using a 10-10-5 plant food; all foliage plants appreciate some feeding at this time of year.

GERANIUMS

This large group of beautiful flowering plants includes zonal, fancy-leaved, ivy, regal, and other types.

Water and Light: Keep soil evenly moist, never soggy, never dry. Geraniums are temperamental about overwatering so be very careful; err on the dry side if anything. Be sure geraniums in this season have some sunlight. They will not bloom without it.

Temperature and Humidity: Geraniums prefer cool temperatures to be their best so try to maintain a range of 65 to 70°F. The plants should not be subject to high humidity. It can do more harm than good. Keep a buoyant atmosphere; stagnant air can create a condition where red spider may attack plants.

Feeding: Adopt a feeding program for geraniums; they do respond well to fertilizer. Once every fourth watering use a 10-10-5 plant food.

Note: These are not easy plants to grow. Success depends on maintaining cool temperatures and growing the plants in an airy place.

GESNERIADS

This group of fine house plants includes African violets, kohlerias, gloxinias, aeschynanthus, rechsteineria, smithiantha, and streptocarpus.

Water and Light: In spring when plants are growing they will require plenty of water, at least twice a week. Keep the soil evenly moist. While some sun is preferred by gesneriads, most will tolerate just bright light and still be healthy.

Temperature and Humidity: Provide good ventilation; a warm flow of air is very beneficial for gesneriads and during this time average home temperatures suit most types. Keep humidity at a 20 to 30 percent level.

Feeding: The gesneriads as a group react favorably to feeding, so use a mild plant food (10-10-5) every third watering. Most gesneriads bloom in summer and fall and are fine accompaniments for orchids. Indeed the gesneriads can be grown quite successfully with orchids.

Note: Gesneriads do need sun in fall and winter to assure bloom, but intense sun in spring and summer can cause leaf scorch. Be prepared to move plants to other locations as the seasons change.

ORCHIDS

These beautiful plants are grown for their flowers; without bloom few orchids are truly handsome. Orchids are seasonal creatures and most must have specific resting periods to encourage flowering. The plants, depending upon the type, bloom in only one season. And in this book you will find orchids that bloom in each.

Water and Light: Orchids, as explained in Chapter 1, are potted in fir bark, and spring-blooming orchids should be flooded with water when you see flower spikes showing. (Do not increase watering until you see spikes showing.) Ample sunlight is necessary to bring buds into bloom, so move plants into sunny places.

Temperature and Humidity: The misconception that orchids need a jungle atmosphere has finally been dispelled; they do quite well in humidity of 30 to 40 percent, but, as with bromeliads, orchids do require good ventilation. Most are air plants and need a fresh buoyant atmosphere, never stagnant. Place plants where there is a constant flow of air.

Feeding: I have grown orchids for twenty-five years and have never given them additional plant food other than a weak solution of fish emulsion once a month during the spring months. Too much feeding can harm orchids because excessive salts become locked into the potting medium; this damages the roots and plants may die.

Note: Some orchids grow all year; others, like coelogyne, dendrobium, laelia, lycaste, and zygopetalum, need a somewhat dry rest for two to three weeks before flowering; then water them while spikes and buds develop and the plant flowers. After blooms fade, rest somewhat dry for four to six weeks. See plant descriptions for specific information on each plant.

PALMS

It's difficult to find better plants for room decoration than palms; there are many kinds to brighten interiors and all are graceful and pretty and offer much for very little care.

Water and Light: Palms start growing in spring, and it is imperative that plants have fresh soil with adequate nutrients. This is the time to increase watering; soil should be evenly moist, almost wet but never soggy. Give plants bright light; intense sun is not necessary. Put palms at west or east windows.

Temperature and Humidity: Palms are flexible as to humidity and temperature requirements; grow in a range of 60 to 80°F and humidity of 10 to 50 percent. Start misting palms at this time of year and wipe leaves with a damp cloth. Plants breathe through their leaves; after a winter of artificial heat when soot and dust may gather on foliage, the damp cloth routine is essential. Don't use any leaf shining preparation. This clogs pores of leaves.

Feeding: If palms are in fresh soil they will not need any feeding, but if they have been in the container a long time — several years — then apply plant food, but sparsely. Use a 10-10-5 fertilizer every fourth watering.

SUCCULENTS

Succulents, which resemble cacti, come in various shapes with exquisite leaf color; some of the echeverias resemble carved jade. As a group these plants are amenable house subjects and add much color to the home.

Water and Light: Unlike the cacti, which generally rest in winter, succulents grow all year, but there still is a seasonal rhythm in their development. In this season most of the plants will be starting a period of growth, so keep soil evenly moist. However, because succulents store water in their leaves, do not water them as much as you would other plants or crown rot or leaf rot may result. Keep plants in a bright place; some sun is fine too.

Temperature and Humidity: Succulents can tolerate a wide range of temperatures but 70 to 75°F is best during the day with a slight drop at night. Average home humidity of 20 to 30 percent is good; never mist succulent plants, because fleshy leaves can rot from lingering water. Be sure air circulation is good; keep windows open slightly or have a small fan operating.

Feeding: If you pot succulents annually, feeding is not necessary. Because many succulents do react unfavorably to plant foods I recommend yearly potting. If, however, you do not have time to repot plants, use a 10-10-5 plant food every third watering during these months.

HOUSE PLANTS FOR SPRING

ABUTILON HYBRIDUM
flowering maple

A tall plant to 30 inches, with maple foliage and pretty pendent paper-thin orange or yellow flowers. Grow in sun and keep soil evenly moist. An easy plant to grow.
Summer: Water heavily, feed moderately. Sun.
Fall: Cut back and repot; keep soil evenly moist. Sun.
Winter: Keep soil evenly moist; mist plant. Sun.

ACACIA ARMATA
kangaroo thorn

This shrub can reach 10 feet outdoors; indoors it will grow to about 36 inches. It has small 1-inch leaves and feathery yellow flower heads. Give moderate or low light; allow soil to dry out between waterings.
All Year: Follow spring schedule.

ACALYPHA HISPIDA
chenille plant

Has rather nice hairy leaves and bright red cattail-type flowers; grows to 24 inches. Needs some sunshine; keep soil evenly moist. A handsome accent for spring cheer.
All Year: Follow spring schedule.

ADIANTUM CAPILLUS VENERIS

This favorite 24-inch fern has wiry black stems adorned with delicate, lacy green fronds. Keep in moderate or low light and be sure soil is evenly moist.
Summer: Flood with water. Moderate light.
Fall: Reduce water somewhat. Bright light.
Winter: Reduce water somewhat. Moderate light.

ADIANTUM TENERUM
maidenhair fern

Another lacy fern that grows to 20 inches. Its distinguished characteristic is lovely pale green fronds that mature to a lush dark green. Give moderate or low light and keep soil evenly moist.
Summer: Flood with water. Keep out of sun.
Fall: Reduce water somewhat. Bright light.
Winter: Keep soil barely moist. Bright light.

AECHMEA CHANTINI

There's nothing nicer for spring beauty than this vase-shaped 30-inch bromeliad with frosty green leaves. Plant bears a thrusting spear of vividly colored bracts with tiny flowers inside. Grow in equal mix of soil and shredded fir bark. Keep the "vase" of the plant filled with water and keep fir bark barely moist. Needs sun.
All Year: Follow spring schedule.

AECHMEA FULGENS

Another lovely vase-shaped bromeliad to 30 inches, with toothed dark-green leaves. The flowers are red tipped with blue. A desirable spring house plant. Give moderate or bright light; keep "vase" filled with water, fir bark evenly moist.
All Year: Follow spring schedule.

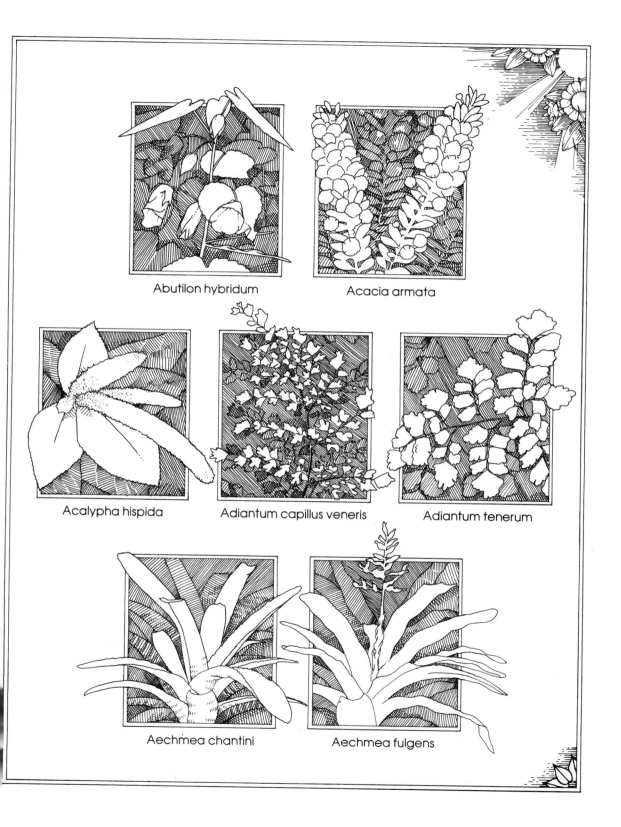

Abutilon hybridum

Acacia armata

Acalypha hispida

Adiantum capillus veneris

Adiantum tenerum

Aechmea chantini

Aechmea fulgens

AERIDES CRASSIFOLIUM

A dependable beautiful orchid that grows to 14 inches. Has straplike dark-green leaves and small, usually spotted, amethyst-purple flowers. This early-spring-blooming orchid needs sunshine. Pot in medium-grade fir bark kept evenly moist. Blooms yearly with little care.

Summer: Reduce moisture somewhat. Move out of sun.
Fall: Keep evenly moist. Place in bright light.
Winter: Increase moisture. Move to sun.

AERIDES FALCATUM

Another handsome orchid, to 20 inches, that bears spring flowers of white and rose. A highly desirable plant; give same treatment as *A. crassifolium.*

Summer: Reduce moisture somewhat. Move out of sun.
Fall: Keep evenly moist. Place in bright light.
Winter: Increase moisture. Move to sun.

ALBUCA MAJOR

Growing to 36 inches, *A. major* has large basal leaves, and erect racemes of pale yellow flowers; a colorful treasure in spring. In fall pot three or four bulbs close together in a 7-inch pot in sandy soil. Give bright light, moderate moisture, until leaves are 6 or 7 inches long; then increase water and place in sun. After plant blooms, let foliage ripen naturally and reduce moisture somewhat; then store pot dry in a shady place until fall. Repot in fresh soil. See Chapter 7 for more information.

ARISTOLOCHIA ELEGANS   calico flower

This fast-growing 60-inch vine makes a fine spring decoration. It has large heart-shaped leaves and bizarre spotted flowers. Flowers form on hanging shoots, so don't cut off. Needs sun and copious watering.

Summer: Water heavily. Sun.
Fall: Needs even moisture. Sun.
Winter: Cut back; repot. Give even moisture. Bright light.

ASCOCENTRUM AMPULLACEUM   carnival orchid

If you want some lovely magenta color indoors at this time of year, grow this fine orchid. It rarely exceeds 20 inches and has strap foliage and many tiny flowers. Needs full sun and copious watering. Grow in fine-grade fir bark.

Summer: Keep evenly moist. No sun.
Fall: Keep evenly moist. Move to sun.
Winter: Dry out somewhat. Sun.

ASCOCENTRUM MINIATUM

This miniature orchid needs only a small space in the window. Although it never grows more than 10 inches, it bears masses of tiny orange flowers. Plant in medium-grade fir bark; give lots of sun and water during growth.

Summer: Keep evenly moist. Keep out of sun.
Fall: Keep evenly moist. Move to sun.
Winter: Dry out somewhat. Sun.

ASPLENIUM NIDUS   birds' nest fern

The popular birds' nest fern is unlike most ferns. With rosette growth, it has broad apple-green leaves and grows to about 18 inches. Place in moderate or low light and keep soil evenly moist.

Summer: Follow spring schedule.
Fall: Follow spring schedule.
Winter: Dry out slightly. Bright light.

Aerides crassifolium

Aerides falcatum

Albuca major

Aristolochia elegans

Ascocentrum ampullaceum

Ascocentrum miniatum

Asplenium nidus

ASPLENIUM VIVIPARUM
spleenwort fern

This handsome 20-inch fern requires bright light and an evenly moist soil. Easy to grow.

Summer: Follow spring schedule.
Fall: Follow spring schedule.
Winter: Dry out slightly. Bright light.

BAMBUSA NANA
miniature bamboo

This is a delightful small-leaved bamboo that grows only 18 inches high. It has the delicate characteristic of bamboo and is splendid green decoration for spring, when color is needed at the window. Grow it in a sunny spot, and be sure to give it plenty of water.

All Year: Follow spring schedule.

BEGONIA CLEOPATRA

A very popular 30-inch begonia; its maple-shaped leaves in variegated colors make this plant especially desirable. It will take sun or shade and needs even moisture; makes a fine hanging plant because it's a halo of color.

All Year: Follow spring schedule.

BEGONIA COCCINEA
angel-wing begonia

A rather tall rangy plant, this begonia has large leaves and is valued for its pendent clusters of delightful small flowers. It requires even moisture and some sun during the day. Otherwise it almost grows by itself. It starts blooming in spring but can continue flowering during the warm months.

All Year: Follow spring schedule.

BEGONIA DREGEI
maple leaf begonia

With oval, angled, and lobed leaves about 3 inches long, this unusual begonia grows to about 18 inches. Although not as spectacular as some begonias, it has a nice compact habit. Allow soil to dry out between waterings; give bright light. Fine dish garden plant.

All Year: Follow spring schedule.

BEGONIA LUXURIANS
palm leaf begonia

Typical of its name, this 18-inch plant has palmlike leaves on erect stems. This plant likes warmth and moderate to low light; give ample water.

Summer: Follow spring schedule.
Fall: Dry out somewhat. Moderate light.
Winter: Keep just barely moist. Bright light.

BEGONIA MASONIANA
iron cross begonia

This popular 16-inch begonia has large somewhat hairy leaves and makes a nice compact plant. Is somewhat touchy about too much moisture at its roots. Avoid sunlight. The leaf color — apple green with a dark cross in center — is beautiful.

Summer: Follow spring schedule.
Fall: Dry out slightly. Moderate light.
Winter: Provide even moisture. Moderate light.

Asplenium viviparum

Bambusa nana

Begonia coccinea

Begonia Cleopatra

Begonia dregei

Begonia luxurians

Begonia masoniana

BEGONIA MAZAE

A small 20-inch begonia with bronze-green satiny leaves, *B. mazae* is a good choice for the beginning gardener. It needs only moderate or low light and an evenly moist soil. Good for terrariums.
All Year: Follow spring schedule.

BEGONIA RICINIFOLIA   castor bean begonia

Resembling the old-fashioned castor bean plant, this begonia grows to 18 inches and has very large green leaves and pretty pink flowers. Dry out between waterings, and place the plant where it will receive moderate or low light. Good plant for artificial light.
All Year: Follow spring schedule.

BEGONIA STRIGILLOSA

With brown-spotted green leaves on graceful stems, this is a handsome small begonia. Needs warmth and even moisture. Blush-white flowers appear at this time of year. Fine for artificial light gardening.
All Year: Follow spring schedule.

BOUGAINVILLEA   paper flower

Popular outdoors and just as good indoors is the old-fashioned favorite bougainvillea, which can grow to 10 feet. Grow it only if you have the space and can give it maximum sunlight. This is a greedy plant that needs lots of watering. It's at its best in summer when flowers appear, but it is attractive in spring because of its leafy look.
Summer: Flood with water. Sun.
Fall: Keep evenly moist. Sun.
Winter: Keep evenly moist. Sun.

CALCEOLARIA   pocketbook plant

This 14-inch annual has little flowers that resemble pocketbooks. You'll find it at nurseries in full bloom, and it provides grand color for the beginning of the year. Unfortunately, it's an annual, so don't try to keep it after the flowers are gone. Grow in sun; keep soil evenly moist.

CHORIZEMA CORDATUM

This member of the pea family is a 36-inch shrub with small ovate leaves and abundant lovely orange-red flowers. The plant requires plenty of sun and even moisture.
Summer: Follow spring schedule.
Fall: Cut back to 10 inches. Provide even moisture. Bright light.
Winter: Provide even moisture. Sun.

CINERARIA

A fine seasonal plant, cineraria is known for its masses of brilliant blue or magenta flowers. Plants to 24 inches are available at nurseries and make lovely color accents in spring. Don't expect more from them though, because they only last the season. The need bright light, evenly moist soil.

Begonia mazae

Begonia ricinifolia

Begonia strigillosa

Bougainvillea

Calceolaria

Chorizema cordatum

Cineraria

CISSUS ANTARCTICA
kangaroo vine

A trailing plant that can grow to 5 feet, *C. antarctica* is fine green color indoors at this time of the year. It has dark-green leaves and is easy to grow. Allow soil to dry out between waterings. An excellent plant for basket growing.
All Year: Follow spring schedule.

CISSUS DISCOLOR
tapestry plant

Not grown as much as the other cissus plants, this one deserves special mention because of its velvety green leaves richly veined with red. Growing to 18 inches, this colorful beauty grows in low or moderate light. Don't overwater. Good basket plant. Grow as cool as possible.
Summer: Keep evenly moist. No sun.
Fall: Dry out somewhat. Low light.
Winter: Allow to dry out between watering. Moderate light.

CISSUS RHOMBIFOLIA
grape ivy

The popular grape ivy, with metallic green-brown leaves, is a natural trailing plant that can reach 10 feet. It seems to withstand almost any condition and still thrive. Not as lush as kangaroo ivy, it's still worth space in the home. Another good basket plant.
Summer: Keep evenly moist. Low light.
Fall: Dry out somewhat. Moderate light.
Winter: Allow to dry out between waterings. Moderate light.

CITRUS TAITENSIS
dwarf orange

A small orange tree at the window in spring is a delightful accent, and this 48-inch plant makes an especially good subject. Give it bright light and allow soil to dry out between waterings. Mist occasionally to keep it looking handsome.
Summer: Follow spring schedule.
Fall: Follow spring schedule.
Winter: Cut back slightly; keep evenly moist. Sun.

CLIVIA MINIATA
kafir lily

Growing from a bulb, this 30-inch plant is elegant in bloom in early April. It bears clusters of truly spectacular orange flowers. Plants bloom best when potbound and will even bear flowers in a shady corner. Water heavily.
See Chapter 7 for more information.

COLUMNEA ARGUTA

A trailer with tiny leaves, this member of the gesneriad family bears bright salmon-red flowers, but not without some pampering. Soil shouldn't be too dry or too wet. Plant will need bright light in summer but all the sun possible in winter. Nice but difficult. Good in baskets or under lights.
Summer: Keep evenly moist. No sun.
Fall: Keep evenly moist. Sun.
Winter: Keep somewhat dry. Sun.

CRASSULA FALCATA

This is an ideal indoor plant, with thick gray sickle-shaped leaves and crowns of orange flowers. Can grow to 30 inches. Seems to thrive in almost any soil or light situation.
Summer: Keep evenly moist.
Fall: Keep evenly moist.
Winter: Dry out between waterings.

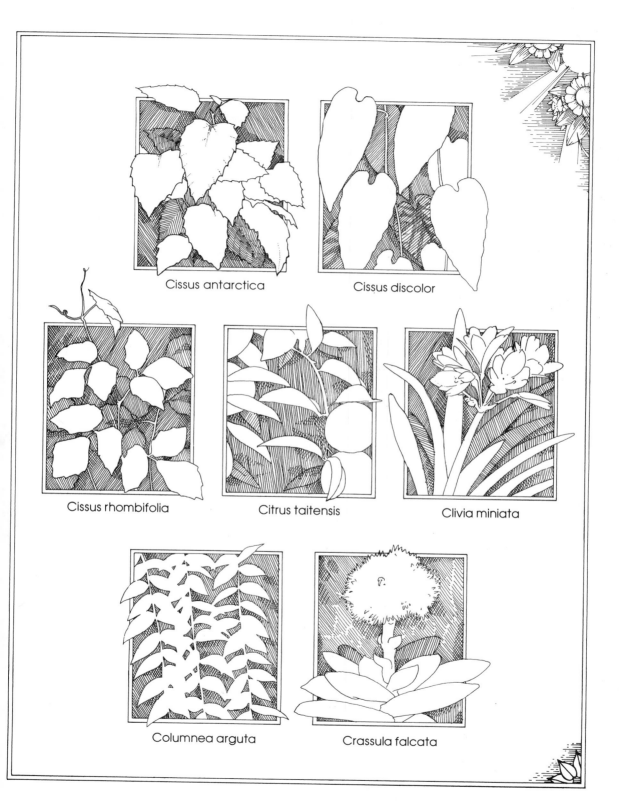

Cissus antarctica

Cissus discolor

Cissus rhombifolia

Citrus taitensis

Clivia miniata

Columnea arguta

Crassula falcata

CRASSULA SCHMIDTII

A miniature crassula, this plant has pointed red-tinted leaves. Grow it in bright light and keep the soil just barely moist. A bushy plant that makes a lovely accent.

All Year: Follow spring schedule.

CROSSANDRA INFUNDIBULIFORMIS

A splendid indoor plant to 28 inches; even small crossandras bear orange flowers on and off through spring and summer. Give the plant sun and good ventilation; nice for the windowsill. Good under lights.

Summer: Water heavily. Sun.
Fall: Keep evenly moist. Sun
Winter: Keep evenly moist. Sun.

CRYPTANTHUS TRICOLOR

A small bromeliad, this species is probably the most popular in the group because of its variegated leaves of white, rose, olive green. The plant requires little attention and needs only moderate or bright light. Pot in fine-grade fir bark. Fine dish garden or terrarium plant.

Summer: Keep evenly moist. Bright light.
Fall: Keep evenly moist. Bright light.
Winter: Dry out slightly. Bright light.

CRYPTANTHUS ZONATUS

This 12-inch bromeliad with wavy brown-green leaves marked with silver is a colorful addition to the spring season. It requires bright light and moderate waterings. Pot in fine-grade fir bark.

Summer: Keep evenly moist. Bright light.
Fall: Keep evenly moist. Sun.
Winter: Dry out slightly. Sun.

CYANOTIS SOMALIENSE   pussy-ears

If you see this 10-inch plant at the florist, buy it, because it's an unusually good house plant. It has triangular glossy green leaves with tiny white hairs. Plants need bright light and plenty of moisture for about a two-month period and then will bear small magenta flowers. Eventually pussy-ears dies down, but don't throw it away. Let it rest for a few months, and then increase moisture to start it into active growth.

Summer: Give plenty of water. Bright light.
Fall: Reduce moisture. Bright light.
Winter: Allow to rest with scanty waterings. Sun.

CYTISUS CANARIENSIS

This is a branching plant to 40 inches. If you give it enough sunlight and some rather copious watering, it might bear yellow flowers.

Summer: Follow spring schedule. Sun.
Fall: Dry out slightly. Sun.
Winter: Keep barely moist. Sun.

DAVALLIA BULLATA MARIESII   rabbit's foot fern

If you like unusual plants, here's one for you. It has unique creepy brown rhizomes that skirt the surface of the soil. The 10-inch fronds are dainty and bright green. For all its beauty, this is a temperamental plant that likes neither too much heat nor too much cold. It requires an evenly moist soil. Nice if you have the time for it. Good for hanging baskets.

Summer: Keep evenly moist. Low light.
Fall: Keep evenly moist. Bright light.
Winter: Dry out between waterings. Bright light.

Crassula schmidtii

Crossandra infundibuliformis

Cryptanthus tricolor

Cryptanthus zonatus

Cyanotis somaliense

Cytisus canariensis

Davallia bullata mariesii

DAVALLIA FEJEENSIS
A feathery 15-inch fern with fluffy leaves, this adds a graceful note indoors. It requires even moisture and low or moderate light.

Summer: Water heavily. Low light.
Fall: Keep evenly moist. Moderate light.
Winter: Keep evenly moist. Moderate light.

DAVALLIA TRICHOMANOIDES
A medium-sized fern to 20 inches, with triangular, rather leathery fronds. This is an arnenable plant that needs bright, moist conditions and provides nice color.

Summer: Water heavily. Low light.
Fall: Keep evenly moist. Moderate light.
Winter: Keep evenly moist. Moderate light.

DENDROBIUM AGGREGATUM   buttercup orchid
A small plant to 14 inches with 6-inch leathery leaves, the buttercup orchid bears its harvest of color in early April. It needs alternating periods of dryness and wetness and as much sun as possible. Grow in medium-grade fir bark.

Summer: Flood with water. Sun.
Fall: Keep evenly moist. Sun.
Winter: Dry out to encourage flowerbuds. Sun.

DENDROBIUM DENSIFLORUM   grape orchid
With clusters of yellow flowers that look like hanging grapes, this 30-inch orchid is dependable for spring. It needs bright sun, good moisture while growing, then a six-week drying-out period after blooming. Pot in medium-grade fir bark.

Summer: Dry out slightly. Sun.
Fall: Increase waterings. Sun.
Winter: Dry out to encourage flower buds. Sun.

DENDROBIUM MOSCHATUM
A deciduous musk-scented flowering orchid, this 30-inch plant bears yellow-rose flowers from April to June. It needs lots of sunlight and water until it blooms, and then a four-week period of scant watering. Resume watering after a month. Grow in large-grade fir bark.

Summer: Dry out slightly. Sun.
Fall: Increase waterings. Sun.
Winter: Dry out to encourage flower buds. Sun.

DENDROBIUM PIERARDII
Blooming on leafless stems, this is an orchid that bears spectacular 5-inch lavender flowers in early April. It's a trailing plant that requires sunlight and should be grown somewhat dry after blooming for about five weeks. Then resume watering to encourage new leaf growth. Pot in fine-grade fir bark.

Summer: Dry out somewhat. Sun.
Fall: Keep evenly moist. Sun.
Winter: Dry out to encourage flower buds. Sun.

DENDROBIUM THYRSIFLORUM
Bearing magnificent 2-inch white and gold flowers in April, this 24-inch orchid needs good sunlight and even moisture until it blooms. After flowers fade, grow somewhat dry for about one month. Give ample sunlight. Pot in large-grade fir bark.

Summer: Dry out somewhat. Sun.
Fall: Keep evenly moist. Sun.
Winter: Dry out to encourage flower buds. Sun.

Davallia fejeensis

Davallia trichomanoides

Dendrobium aggregatum

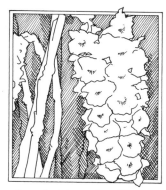

Dendrobium densiflorum

Dendrobium moschatum

Dendrobium pierardii

Dendrobium thyrsiflorum

DIEFFENBACHIA AMOENA — dumbcane

A popular dieffenbachia, this plant grows to 36 inches, with green and white foliage. It thrives in low light and needs plenty of water.

Summer: Follow spring schedule.
Fall: Follow spring schedule.
Winter: Dry out between waterings. Bright light.

DIEFFENBACHIA EXOTICA

This lovely multicolored foliage plant with broad leaves grows to about 36 inches. *D. exotica* needs bright light and plenty of moisture except in winter, when it should be grown barely moist.

Summer: Follow spring schedule.
Fall: Follow spring schedule.
Winter: Dry out between waterings. Bright light.

DIEFFENBACHIA PICTA

Green leaves dotted white make this 36-inch plant a handsome addition to the indoor garden. It's one of the most amenable dieffenbachias and grows well in most light and soil situations. Keep evenly moist.

Summer: Follow spring schedule.
Fall: Follow spring schedule.
Winter: Dry out between waterings. Bright light.

EPIDENDRUM ATROPURPUREUM

A popular orchid, this plant has egg-shaped pseudobulbs and grows to 30 inches. It bears dozens of 1-inch brown and purple flowers in May, sometimes earlier. It needs ample sun and even moisture. Pot in medium-grade fir bark.

Summer: Dry out slightly. Sun.
Fall: Provide ample water. Sun.
Winter: Dry out slightly to encourage flower buds. Sun.

EPIDENDRUM FRAGRANS

With fragrant magenta flowers, this late-spring-blooming orchid grows to 24 inches. It likes full sunlight and even moisture. Grow in medium-grade fir bark.

All Year: Follow spring schedule.

EPIDENDRUM O'BRIENIANUM

Growing like a weed, this tall reed-stemmed orchid bears clusters of tiny pink or orange flowers throughout the spring months. Needs copious watering and full sunlight to be at its best.

Summer: Follow spring schedule.
Fall: Provide even moisture. Sun.
Winter: Provide even moisture. Sun.

EPIDENDRUM STAMFORDIANUM

With egg-shaped pseudobulbs and single leathery leaves, *E. stamfordianum* bears clusters of yellow and yellow-red flowers in early spring. This orchid requires much moisture until bloom time comes, but then give it moderate watering. Does best in bright light.

Summer: Follow spring schedule. Sun.
Fall: Follow spring schedule. Sun.
Winter: Dry out severely. Sun.

Dieffenbachia amoena

Dieffenbachia exotica

Dieffenbachia picta

Epidendrum atropupureum

Epidendrum fragrans

Epidendrum O'Brienianum

Epidendrum stamfordianum

EUCHARIS GRANDIFLORA
Amazon lily

A desirable glossy green, 40-inch bulbous plant, *E. grandiflora* bears fragrant white flowers. It is generally available as a pot plant this time of year and needs bright light and plenty of water. After it blooms, keep it rather dry for a few weeks and then start the cycle again.

Summer: Dry out slightly. No sun.
Fall: Increase waterings. Sun.
Winter: Dry out slightly. Sun.

FICUS BENJAMINA
weeping fig

A popular indoor tree, this branching 48-inch plant has small oval leaves. It needs even moisture and bright light. In fall it sheds leaves but produces a new crop within a few months.

Summer: Follow spring schedule.
Fall: Follow spring schedule.
Winter: Dry out between waterings. Bright light.

FICUS DIVERSIFOLIA
mistletoe fig

Growing to 24 inches, this branching plant has lovely round leaves and grows with little care. Give it even moisture and bright light. Good under lights or in dish gardens or terrariums.

Summer: Follow spring schedule.
Fall: Follow spring schedule.
Winter: Dry out between waterings. Bright light.

FICUS ELASTICA
rubber plant

This popular plant can grow to 5 feet, and has thick glossy green leaves. It requires bright light and an evenly moist soil.

Summer: Follow spring schedule.
Fall: Follow spring schedule.
Winter: Dry out between waterings. Sun.

FICUS LYRATA
fiddleleaf fig

With enormous 36-inch leaves, the fiddleleaf fig can grow to 5 feet indoors. It's somewhat temperamental, however, and can't tolerate temperature fluctuations. It needs bright light and even moisture.

Summer: Follow spring schedule.
Fall: Follow spring schedule.
Winter: Dry out between waterings. Low light.

GAZANIA

Here's an annual garden flower that will bloom indoors in bright sunlight. It has black-eyed orange daisy blooms and woolly gray-green foliage. Plants bloom on and off through spring and into summer but need lots of water and plenty of sunlight.

GUZMANIA MONOSTACHIA
red-hot-poker-plant

A small bromeliad to 18 inches, this one has straplike green leaves and bears a poker-shaped flower head of red, black, and white in spring or in fall. The plant requires little care other than even moisture and bright light. Grow in equal parts soil and fine-grade fir bark. Fine for artificial-light gardens.

Summer: Provide ample water. Sun.
Fall: Keep evenly moist. Sun.
Winter: Keep evenly moist. Sun.

Eucharis grandiflora

Ficus benjamina

Ficus diversifolia

Ficus elastica

Ficus lyrata

Gazania

Guzmania monostachia

HAEMANTHUS KATHERINAE   blood lily
A very ornamental 30-inch bulb plant, with hundreds of tiny flowers in a spike, *H. katherinae* is a stellar indoor subject. Pot one bulb with top protruding in a 5 or 7-inch container. Give it plenty of water and sun.
See Chapter 7 for more information.

HAEMANTHUS MULTIFLORUS   blood lily
Don't let this plant fool you. It bears its red flowers in spring before leaves develop. It grows to about 20 inches and needs lots of sun and even moisture. Tough to find but worth the search.
See Chapter 7 for more information.

HELICONIA PSITTICORUM   parrot flower
A member of the banana family, this 36-inch plant has rich green leaves, orange bracts, and greenish-yellow flowers. Give sun and keep soil evenly moist; makes a good indoor decoration.
Summer: Follow spring schedule.
Fall: Follow spring schedule.
Winter: Dry out between waterings. Sun.

HYDRANGEA
This is a popular Easter pot plant, with large leaves and showy clusters of white, blue, or pink flowers. Keep soil almost wet and grow cool in sun with plenty of fresh air. After plants bloom, remove from pot and cut back shoots to two joints; repot plant outdoors. Many varieties available.

IXORA CHINENSIS   flame-of-the-woods
A robust house plant to 36 inches, *I. chinensis* has small dark-green leaves and clusters of bright flowers that appear in early spring into summer. Plants need sun and a moist soil.
Summer: Follow spring schedule. Sun.
Fall: Follow spring schedule. Sun.
Winter: Dry out between waterings. Sun.

LYCASTE AROMATICA   cinnamon orchid
A small orchid, to 24 inches, with broad green leaves and lovely butter-yellow flowers, *L. aromatica* needs good sunlight and plenty of water when growing. After it blooms, dry plant out somewhat for about one month.
Summer: Dry out severely. Cooler temperatures. Bright light.
Fall: Resume watering. Sun.
Winter: Keep evenly moist. Sun.

LYCASTE SKINNERI
This national flower of Guatamala has large blush-white flowers. The plant grows to about 24 inches and needs bright light and rather heavy watering until bloom time. After flowers fade, carry plant somewhat dry for about two months.
Summer: Keep evenly moist. Low light.
Fall: Dry out severely; cooler temperatures. Bright light.
Winter: Keep evenly moist. Sun.

Haemanthus katherinae

Haemanthus multiflorus

Heliconia psitticorum

Hydrangea

Ixora chinensis

Lycaste aromatica

Lycaste skinneri

MUSA VELUTINA
banana plant

Growing to 36 inches, the banana plant has shiny green spatula leaves and makes a fine indoor decoration. Give sun and an evenly moist soil.

Summer: Flood with water. Sun.
Fall: Keep evenly moist. Sun.
Winter: Keep evenly moist. Sun.

NEPHROLEPIS BOSTONIENSE
Boston fern

This plant requires little introduction. It's fast growing, to about 36 inches, and has feathery green fronds. Give bright light and keep soil evenly moist, but avoid overwatering. Fine basket plant.

Summer: Give ample water. No sun.
Fall: Keep evenly moist. Bright light.
Winter: Keep evenly moist. Bright light.

NOTOCACTUS OTTONIS
ball cactus

A fine miniature cactus, this is a 2-inch ribbed globe that bears large yellow flowers. The plant needs sun and a moderately moist soil. If any cactus will bloom indoors, this one will. Good under lights.

Summer: Give ample water. Sun.
Fall: Keep evenly moist. Sun.
Winter: Dry out somewhat; provide cool place (65° F). Bright light.

NOTOCACTUS SCOPA

To 8 inches in diameter, *N. scopa* is covered with white hairs and bears large flowers. Like most cacti it needs good sunlight and moderately moist soil. This one will be with you for a long time no matter how you treat it.

Summer: Give ample water. Sun.
Fall: Keep evenly moist. Sun.
Winter: Dry out somewhat; provide cool place (65° F). Bright light.

ORNITHOGALUM ARABICUM

A fine bulbous plant to 24 inches, *O. arabicum* has grassy foliage and clusters of white flowers with black centers — flowers are excellent for cutting. Grow in full sun and keep plants evenly moist. You'll have to start the plant from a bulb. Put six or seven bulbs in a 6-inch container in September for flowers this season. After flowers fade, let soil dry out naturally, and then store plants in their pots in a cool shady place for three months. Repot in fresh soil for a new harvest of bloom.

See Chapter 7 for more information.

PASSIFLORA CAERULEA
passion flower

This vining plant, to 60 inches, has lobed leaves and incredible large dark-blue and pink flowers. Not an easy plant to grow indoors. It requires space, buckets of water, and good sun. After plants bloom, rest plants somewhat dry for three months and then restart the passion vine in fresh soil. Cut back to 4 inches at restarting time.

PASSIFLORA TRIFASCIATA
passion flower

Not as popular as *P. caerulea,* this is another fine vining plant to 60 inches, with glowing purple and green foliage and blue flowers. It too needs plenty of space, good sun, and ample water. Treat like *P. caerulea.*

Musa velutina

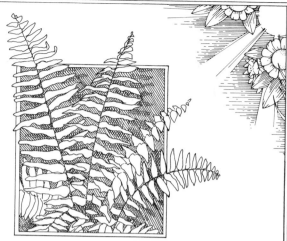

Nephrolepis Bostoniense

Notocactus ottonis

Notocactus scopa

Ornithogalum arabicum

Passiflora caerulea

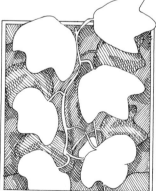

Passiflora trifasciata

PELARGONIUM 'BETTER TIMES'   geranium

A fine 24-inch geranium that bears red flowers, 'Better Times' makes an
excellent indoor plant. It requires even moisture and bright light.

Summer: Keep evenly moist; as cool as possible. Low light.
Fall: Keep evenly moist. Bright light.
Winter: Dry out somewhat. Sun.

PELARGONIUM 'SALMON SPLENDOR'

Known for its beautiful pastel coloring, this popular 24-inch geranium needs
winter sun and summer shade and ample moisture.

Summer: Keep evenly moist; as cool as possible. Low light.
Fall: Keep evenly moist. Bright light.
Winter: Dry out somewhat. Sun essential.

PELARGONIUM 'SKIES OF ITALY'

A 20-inch geranium grown for its exquisite foliage, 'Skies of Italy' has pink and
green and yellow-edged leaves. It is one of the popular zonal geraniums and
needs coolness and ample moisture.

Summer: Keep evenly moist; as cool as possible. Low light.
Fall: Keep evenly moist. Bright light.
Winter: Dry out somewhat. Sun essential.

PETREA VOLUBILIS   queen's wreath

A vining plant, to 60 inches, queen's wreath has spectacular blue flowers
now. This is a big plant that grows rapidly and needs space. It needs full sun;
let soil dry out between waterings. Have patience with petrea; only 3 or
4-year-old plants bloom well.

Summer: Follow spring schedule.
Fall: Follow spring schedule.
Winter: Dry out between waterings. Sun.

PHOENIX ROEBELENII   date palm

Phoenix is a fine palm for indoors, growing to 40 inches. It has stiff dark-green
leaves and a nice branching habit. Grow it in bright or moderate light, and
allow soil to dry out between waterings. Really an amenable plant, phoenix
offers much pleasure for little effort.

Summer: Follow spring schedule.
Fall: Keep evenly moist. Bright light.
Winter: Dry out between waterings. Bright light.

RHAPIS EXCELSA   lady palm

This robust palm with fan fronds on cane stems grows to 40 inches. It needs
bright light; allow soil to dry out between waterings. Unlike most palms,
which are tall and branching, the lady palm is compact and lush, a splendid
green accent for spring.

Summer: Water heavily. Bright light.
Fall: Keep evenly moist. Bright light.
Winter: Dry out between waterings. Sun.

RHAPIS HUMILIS

Not as popular as *R. excelsa* and smaller in size, *R. humilis* is somewhat more
graceful in branching habit. It needs low or moderate light; allow soil to dry
out between waterings.

Summer: Water heavily. Moderate light.
Fall: Keep soil evenly moist. Moderate light.
Winter: Dry out between waterings. Bright light.

Pelargonium 'Better Times'

Pelargonium 'Salmon Splendor'

Pelargonium 'Skies of Italy'

Petrea volubilis

Phoenix roebelenii

Rhapis excelsa

Rhapis humilis

RHOEO DISCOLOR
Moses-in-a-boat

An unusual small plant, rhoeo has olive-green lance-shaped leaves that are purple underneath, with tiny white flowers at base of leaves. It needs bright light but little sun, and ample moisture. Good under lights.

Summer: Keep evenly moist. Low light.
Fall: Keep evenly moist. Low light.
Winter: Dry out somewhat. Sun.

ROSA CHINENSIS MINIMA
miniature rose

Some people can grow miniature roses with tremendous success; others find them difficult. The plants are tiny replicas of large roses and grow to about 14 inches. Flowers come in many colors. Miniature roses need ample sun as well as a cool place. Many varieties are available, and you could make a full-time hobby of growing these lilliputian delights.

Summer: Give ample moisture. Sun.
Fall: Keep evenly moist. Sun.
Winter: Dry out somewhat. Sun.

SASA PYGMAEA
miniature bamboo

A grassy plant growing to 14 inches, sasa is really a fine indoor subject overlooked by most gardeners. It's bushy, green, and pretty and needs little care. Give it copious water and a bright place; it will take care of itself.

All Year: Follow spring schedule.

SPREKELIA FORMOSISSIMA
Jacobean lily

Sprekelia bears magnificent red flowers in April. This 20-inch plant grows from a bulb; flowers appear before foliage. Pot one bulb to one 6-inch pot in late winter. Set in a sunny window and keep soil evenly moist from time growth starts until September; then carry somewhat dry until December or January. See Chapter 7 for more information.

STEPHANOTIS FLORIBUNDA
Madagascar jasmine

This lovely plant starts blooming in late winter and into February. Growing to 60 inches or more, stephanotis has green leathery leaves and heavily scented white flowers. It needs plenty of water until flowers appear; then it can be carried somewhat dry. For best results, grow Madagascar jasmine very cool (60° F); perhaps you can put it in an unheated but not freezing area of the home. Difficult but well worth the effort.

Summer: Give ample moisture. No sun.
Fall: Keep evenly moist; as cool as possible. Sun.
Winter: Dry out between waterings; keep cool. Sun.

STROBILANTHES ISOPHYLLUS

A plant not often seen, strobilanthes grows to 24 inches and has willowy leaves and blue and white flowers. It needs sun and plenty of water and will be good for only one season, but you can take cuttings for new plants for the following year.

VALLOTA SPECIOSA
Scarborough lily

Vallota is a large, bulbous, 24-inch plant with clusters of funnel-form red flowers in late spring. In fall, place a bulb in a small pot (4 or 5 inches); crowded roots induce good blooming. Be sure the point of the bulb is just below the surface of the soil. Grow in a sunny place and keep soil moderately moist except after flowering; then grow not quite so wet for about five weeks, but never dry out completely. A spectacular plant.

See Chapter 7 for more information.

Rhoeo discolor

Rosa chinensis minima

Sasa pygmaea

Sprekelia formosissima

Stephanotis floribunda

Strobilanthes isophyllus

Vallota speciosa

PART TWO

SUMMER

4 TENDING THE INDOOR GARDEN IN SUMMER

IN THIS WARMEST SEASON of the year, every-other-day watering and some feeding are vital because now plants are really growing. And now you must do something to keep down heat, which can desiccate plants, and to maintain a buoyant atmosphere in the growing area.

GROWING-ON

"Growing-on" simply means that the seedlings you started in February and March are doing well and making steady growth; fresh leaves are unfurling and new stems sprouting. If any of these youngsters are sulking, give them special attention. Put them in a window greenhouse if you have one, or in another location; sometimes moving plants a few inches makes all the difference. Mist the growing areas with water, keep the soil evenly moist, and watch daily for pests. If the leaves are wilted, put the plants in a special area that is cool at night and always has good air circulation.

If there seems to be no apparent reason why some of the young plants aren't doing well, unpot them and look at roots to be sure they're actively growing — white roots signify a healthy plant. Brown-tipped roots are dead; trim back and repot in fresh soil and try again.

Although sunlight is beneficial for most plants during the spring, fall, and especially winter, in the summer, sunlight hitting glass panes

In summer, plants make fast growth; this handsome group of house plants is at its peak. (Photo by Matthew Barr)

will be reflected onto plant leaves and may burn foliage. This is especially true if your plants are at a south or west window; provide protection in the form of a light curtain or trellis work applied to the window. Wooden trellis screens help distribute the light on plants and shade the area so the room is cooled. If you can't install trellises or have curtains at windows, just move the plants farther back into room away from direct sun.

TEMPERATURE AND VENTILATION

When days get hot, all we can do is keep the air conditioner going. And air conditioning does help plants live more comfortably. However, nighttime temperature difference is beneficial for plants; night temperatures should be lower than daytime ones by about 10 to 15 degrees. Air conditioners don't allow the free circulation of outdoor air that plants like, and if the machines are on all day and night, night temperatures will stay constant.

Years ago I had an air-conditioned apartment, and my plants showed no exceptional increase of growth as did the ones I grew later in non-air-conditioned rooms. Plants in air-conditioned rooms don't die, but they don't grow too much either, so if possible grow your plants in rooms without air conditioners. Besides protecting plants from sun and heat, you *must* keep a flow of fresh air in the growing areas. Few plants, whether indoors or out, survive long in stagnant conditions. Keep windows open whenever possible, and direct a small oscillating fan (at low speed) at the ceiling above the growing area. The fan will keep air moving constantly and thus furnish a buoyant atmosphere, which plants like.

Ventilation is important in summer. Air must be kept circulating to keep plants healthy, and some protection from direct sun is needed. Shutters are used in this window garden. (Photo by Jerry Bagger)

SUMMERING PLANTS OUTDOORS

Most plants benefit from outdoor rains and fresh air currents, but some do not, and in fact will suffer from the transition from indoor to outdoor summer conditions. Ferns, palms, and other low-light-level plants like grape ivy, philodendrons, and Chinese evergreens should stay indoors all year. They don't need the additional light outdoors. Vining plants and large plants are a chore to move and palms can be ruined in a wind storm. On the other hand, many flowering plants — gesneriads, orchids, bromeliads — appreciate a summer outdoors. If you put plants outdoors in summer (from June through September) different watering and feeding schedules are needed. Let's look at outdoor summer care for plants.

A prime reason for summering plants outdoors is to enable them to restore themselves and gather vigor for the coming seasons (just as you take a vacation now and then to revive your energies). The healthier the plant is by the end of the summer, the more apt it is to go through the dull months ahead without incident, such as insect attack or limp growth from overwatering or underwatering.

On gravel in pans, plants are assured of more humidity; gravel should be kept moist, especially in summer when heat is high. (Photo by Molly Adams)

Bromeliads are summered outdoors so they can benefit from rain and good air circulation. It is a simple matter to move small and medium-sized plants outside; larger plants of course are a chore. (Photo by Matthew Barr)

A patio area that's partially shaded is a fine place for potted plants to reside over summer — they benefit from the outdoor conditions and the patio benefits from the fresh green color. Another excellent summering place for plants is under trees, where they are protected from intense overhead light and heavy winds and storms.

Outdoors, it's much better to leave plants in pots rather than uprooting and planting them in the ground. Roots are disturbed and can grow wild. Leave plants in their pots and elevate them on bricks or pieces of wood so air reaches the underside of the pots and insects don't have too easy a time getting to the plants.

If possible, hang plants from rafters and beams of porches. Plants at eye level look good and benefit from air on all sides. Again, don't unpot anything; merely use the plant hangers that clip onto the rim of the pot and a chain suspended from an eye hook. Colorful geraniums, trailing columneas, and the like can decorate any area outdoors.

Plants can be slipped into decorative containers to provide beauty outdoors and then moved inside when weather becomes inclement. (Photo by Matthew Barr)

If you're an apartment dweller, don't miss the opportunity of putting plants outdoors. Secure an inexpensive plastic windowbox to the sill so your plants can be seen from inside while they bask in outdoor conditions. House and garage roofs are other areas to place plants for summer, and a few plants can decorate the back doorstep. When I was in an apartment in Chicago I always summered some plants on the back porch. If you live in a high-rise, summer plants on the balconies.

Outdoors, natural air currents dry out plants quickly. If it doesn't rain too often, you'll have to water your plants — every-other-day watering is almost essential. And just as you soak plants indoors when you water them, soak them outside too. Plants really can use a great deal of water when weather is warm and light is at a maximum. Be sure to water the foliage too. Feed plants outdoors with a slightly heavier concentration of plant food than you would use indoors.

Outdoors, plants are more liable to be attacked by insects because there are more insects outdoors on neighboring trees and shrubs. Spray plants with an insecticide once while they are outdoors. (This is one time I do use pesticides.)

In most parts of the country you'll have to take indoor plants inside in mid-September because some plants can be harmed if temperature drops to, say, 55°F. Before you bring in your plants, be sure they harbor no insects. Make an eye inspection, and hose them down thoroughly. Once the plants are inside, keep watching them for a few days to be sure no outdoor insects hitched a ride for an indoor vacation.

When you get plants into the house after their outdoor sojourn don't panic if they lose a few leaves or seem limp. This is a natural condition as plants adjust to indoor conditions. Eventually, they will perk up and be as good as ever.

VACATION CARE

If you have many house plants, when your vacation time comes you wonder who will take care of the indoor greenery. No one can do it as well as you can, but some provisions must be made so that plants survive while you're gone.

Rooftops or garage tops provide an excellent place to summer plants. (Photo by Matthew Barr)

Most plants can survive a weekend without harm if you set up vacation-watering methods before you leave. If you're going away for more than a few days, then you must use other methods to keep your plants growing. These can range from mechanical devices — self-watering pots and wicks — to hiring a plant sitter to come in and tend plants.

Except for a few plants like piggybacks, coleus, and crotons, which need buckets of water, most plants can survive for a weekend, *if* you prepare beforehand.

Thoroughly water plants in very large pots before you leave (large pots hold water longer than small ones). If your plants are in 3 to 5-inch pots, the soil will dry out quickly, so prepare a small metal bin or plastic tray (5 or 6 inches deep and watertight) with a 2 to 3-inch bed of gravel. Pour water into the tray until it just reaches the top of the gravel, and set the potted plants on top of the gravel. Now wrap and pack sphagnum moss or newspapers around the outsides of the

If you go away for a few days you can leave plants in a saucer of water; elevate them on a brick with water level to the top of the brick. This way the brick pulls up water and provides some additional moisture for plants. (Photo by Matthew Barr)

Here a plant has been wrapped in wet newspapers; water has been left in the saucer and the plant will be all right for three to five days. (Photo by Matthew Barr)

pots, to within 2 inches of the pot rim. Moisten the moss or newspaper; this method will keep plants moist for several days. If you don't want to bother with a bin, use the bathtub — instead of gravel, set plants on standard house bricks. Fill the tub with enough water to reach the top of the bricks.

Soak medium-sized plants in 8 to 12-inch containers thoroughly the morning you leave. Mist leaves with water to refresh them; these plants should stay moist for four to five days. If you're a worrier, set these plants on bricks in tubs.

If you're going away for a week or more, the ideal solution is to have a friend or relative come to water the plants. But often this isn't possible, and that's when the plant-watering devices are handy. Self-watering pots work well for small pots. (As yet the self-watering pot for large plants in 8 or 10-inch pots hasn't been introduced.) Simply fill the water reservoirs at the bottom of the pots; wicks or other water-releasing devices then supply water slowly to the soil, furnishing moisture for plants for about one week. Check the directions for the pots you buy, because there are several brands, and each has its

67

If you are away for a few days you can leave a plant wrapped in wet sphagnum as shown here. Sphagnum holds water and releases moisture over a long period of time. (Photo by Matthew Barr)

own set of rules. Unfortunately, these pots are an expensive way to keep plants watered if you have a dozen or more plants. In fact, it's *too* expensive, but you can devise your own water-releasing systems. This is not as difficult as you might think; use plastic bins and buy wicks from plant suppliers.

What do you do with the larger plants if you can't get anyone to come in? The only alternative is to use one of the inexpensive plant waterers. One device has worked quite well for me: you fill the oval ball and insert the waterer into the soil; water is released slowly over a period of time. I found that the water lasted for about five days, which is ample time if you're gone a week, since two days without water won't kill most plants.

Because plants have become a part of almost every American home, the business of plant sitting is thriving. If you know youngsters in the neighborhood who need some extra money, have them water plants while you're on a long vacation. Or have a greenhouse in your area take care of plants. Many florists and nurseries will board your plants, but you must deliver them to the place.

Watering plants is of prime importance if you go away, but heat and light must also be considered. If you close all the shades and blinds, your house will be dark and plants will suffer greatly. Allow some natural light to enter so the plants can grow. Group all plants at the windows where the best light comes in; you can then shutter the rest of the windows.

Excessive heat can kill plants, especially in the summer. If the house is closed tight as a drum, heat will accumulate. Yet you don't want to leave windows open because this is an invitation to burglars. The best you can do in this situation is hope that the weather doesn't turn broiling hot. If you live in an area with very hot summers, you *must* make other arrangements for plants, such as taking them to a nursery.

If you're vacationing during the winter, set the thermostat at 65°F; most plants will get along well at this temperature.

5 PESTS AND DISEASES

INSECTS

THE BEAUTY of indoor greenery is admired not only by you but also by insects. To you, plants are a visual treat, but they're a gastronomical treat to bugs. Not too many insects will bother your plants, but there will be occasional visitors. Some you can get rid of quickly; others you can't, no matter what precautions you take. Pest problems will be minimal in the winter; insects are more apt to proliferate in the early summer, because the warmer the weather, the more broods of insects are hatched. But insects are really no problem if you tackle them early. Left to multiply, insects cause havoc in the indoor garden, so observation is nine-tenths of the battle.

I've grown hundreds of house plants in the last fifteen years — at windows, in terrariums, in hanging containers — and by far the most pesky pests are mealybugs, those white, cottony, waxy devils that seem to multiply overnight. And indeed they do: each mealybug is capable of giving birth to 600 in forty-eight hours!

Red spider occasionally attacks my plants, but only when I forget to keep them moist in hot dry spells. No matter how careful you are, aphids (plant lice) will bother plants if you don't kill the bugs *early*. Other house plant pests are whiteflies, thrips, snails, and scale, an armored-tank type of insect that attaches to plant stems and sucks plant juices. Scale can be a bother, but they aren't as persistent as mealybugs.

Most of the pests I have mentioned are recognizable on sight (except the red spider, but you'll see their webs). Here's an easy description of each pest that might bother your house plants:

Aphids: Pear-shaped, small, soft-bodied insects with beaks and four needlelike stylets. Brown, red, green, or yellow in color.

Mealybugs: Cottony waxlike insects with segmented bodies.

Red spider mites: Tiny and oval yellow-green, red, or brown creatures.

Thrips: Chewing, small and slender, dark-colored insects with two pairs of wings.

Snails: You'll know them when you see them.

Let's see what each pest does to a plant so you'll be able to recognize its work if you don't see the insect the first time around:

Aphids: Plants lose vigor and become stunted; leaves curl or pucker.

Mealybugs: Leaves wilt; young growth is stunted.

Red spider mites: Foliage becomes pale and stippled.
Scale: Leaf and stem damage.
Thrips: Silver sheen on the leaves.
Snails: Holes eaten in leaves.

PREVENTATIVES

Now you know the culprits and what they do (but only what they do if you don't catch them early). If you're on your toes and daily observe your plants, damage will be minimal even if insects are present. If you see the insects on a few leaves, discard the leaves. However, in most cases some more precaution must be taken, which means old-fashioned methods (preferably) or chemicals (if natural methods don't work and you don't mind using chemicals).

Scale attaches itself to leaf surfaces; the small spots you see on the leaves can be eliminated without difficulty if caught early. (Photo by Matthew Barr)

Old-Fashioned Remedies

The first line of defense against insects is old-fashioned remedies. Believe me, these methods work quite well, and you won't have to keep poisons in the house. Try these cures:

1. *Laundry soap and water.* Mix half a bar of a laundry soap like Ivory with 5 quarts of water. Dip a cotton swab into the mixture and either dab the insects or, at the sink, pour the soap and water mixture over the plant. Then rinse the plant with tepid water. Repeat at least at three-day intervals.
2. *Alcohol.* Alcohol on a cotton swab applied directly to mealybugs and aphids will kill them. Make repeated applications.
3. *Tobacco.* Just as bad for insects as it is for human beings. Steep old tobacco from cigarettes in water for several days to make a solution that will get rid of scale. Repeat every third day.
4. *Hand-picking.* Not for the queasy. Hand-pick with a toothpick.
5. *Wiping.* Wipe leaves with a damp cloth dipped in plain water. This will eliminate eggs before they hatch.
6. *Water spray.* This may sound ineffective, but if you persist, it works on many insects. Use a strong spray of water at the sink.

Mealybugs—white cottony insects—especially gather on the undersides of veined plants. This infestation has gotten a good start and may be difficult to eliminate quickly. (Photo by Matthew Barr)

Insecticides

Some people question the use of chemicals in the home, and rightly so. They should be avoided. However, some of the natural preventatives that contain pyrethrum or rotenone are generally safe for home use.

Insecticides are available in many forms, with the granular (both standard and systemic types) the most convenient to use: just sprinkle granules on the soil and apply water. Water-soluble insecticides are sprayed on plants with special sprayers. Powders or dusts, to my way of thinking, are not necessary in the home. Systemics also are gaining popularity. Systemics — insecticides applied directly to the soil — are very convenient to use. Systemics are granules; you spread them on the soil and then thoroughly water the plant. The insecticide is drawn up through the roots into the sap stream, making the sap toxic. Thus when sucking and chewing insects start dining on the plant, they're poisoned. Systemics protect plants from most, but not all, sucking and chewing pests for six to eight weeks, so generally you have to apply this type of insecticide only three or four times a year to protect plants.

You should know where to look for insects, because they attack various parts of plants. Most insects lurk in leaf axils and on the undersides of leaves. Scrutinize these places carefully with a magnifying glass if necessary. Thrips hide in soil, and snails hide under pots. Scale almost exclusively cling to stems at the lower part of a plant.

Delicate leafy plants are more prone to attack than heavy-leaved ones. It's a good idea to really get ready for summer by washing plants at the sink with a strong spray of water. Gently massage axils with water, and then wipe leaves so they're shiny and clean of soot, dust, and spores that might harbor enemies.

Another important procedure for insect prevention, especially in summer, is to soak pots in the sink in water up to the pot rim; if any insects are lingering in the soil, they'll come to the surface after a few hours, at which time you can battle them.

If you use commercial preparations, do follow the directions to the letter. Usually repeated doses are necessary to eliminate insects. And do keep all commercial preparations out of the reach of children and pets. Whichever method you use—commercial safe preparations, or old-fashioned remedies—follow these six rules:

1. Never use a chemical on a bone-dry plant.
2. Never spray plants in direct sun.
3. Use sprays at the proper distance marked on the package.
4. Try to douse insects if they're in sight.
5. Don't use chemicals on ferns.
6. Always use chemicals in well-ventilated areas; outdoors is good.

This wax plant has a conglomerate of disease and mealy bug invasion and needs severe pruning and treatment. (Photo by Matthew Barr)

PLANT DISEASES

If plants are well cared for, they rarely develop diseases. But no one wants a costly plant ruined by fungus or botrytis, so a little knowledge about plant diseases can help you save infected plants. Most house plant diseases are minor if treated early, but if left unchecked they become major killers.

You'll be able to tell if plants are hit by diseases by such visible symptoms as spots, rot, and mildew. Many plant diseases cause similar external symptoms, so you must identify the specific disease to be sure you use the correct cure. Your state agricultural agent is your best source of help. Too little or too much humidity or too much feeding can help cause disease, but diseases are mainly caused by bacteria and fungi. Bacteria enter the plant through its naturally minute wounds and small openings. Inside, bacteria multiply and start to break down plant tissue. Animals, soil, insects, water, and dust carry bacteria that can attack plants. And if you've touched a diseased plant, you too can carry the disease to healthy plants. Soft roots, leaf spots, wilts, and rots are some diseases caused by bacteria.

A closeup of mealybugs; they have already caused the plant to lose leaves.
(Photo by Matthew Barr)

This peperomia has mealybugs; note the cupped stunted leaves at upper left.
(Photo by Matthew Barr)

Fungi, like bacteria, enter a plant through a wound or a natural opening or by forcing their entrance directly through plant stems or leaves. Spores are carried by wind, water, insects, people, and equipment. Fungi multiply rapidly in shady, damp conditions rather than in hot, dry situations, because moisture is essential in their reproduction. Fungi cause rusts, mildew, some leaf spots, and blights.

FUNGICIDES

Fungicides are chemicals that kill or inhibit the growth of bacteria and fungi. They come in ready-to-use dust form, in wettable powder, or in soluble forms that mix with water and are sprayed on. Here's a brief résumé of the many fungicides available:

Captan: A fungicide that's generally safe and effective for the control of many diseases.

Ferbam: A very effective fungicide against rusts.

Karanthane: Highly effective for many types of powdery mildew.

Sulfur: This is an old and inexpensive fungicide and still good; it controls many diseases.

Zineb: Used for many bacterial and fungous diseases.

Benomyl: A systemic used for certain bacterial and fungous diseases.

6 WHAT TO DO IN SUMMER

BEGONIAS

Lush foliage and cascades of flowers are your reward if you treat begonias properly; in summer many start blooming profusely.

Water and Light: Increase watering and put the plants where there is ample light or some sun. Warmth (over 80°F) should not harm the plants; most thrive on heat. (Exceptions are rex begonias; keep shaded.) Keep soil evenly moist but be careful with rhizomatous begonias; water on the scandent rhizomes can cause rot.

Temperature and Humidity: Provide ample ventilation (all begonias appreciate a fresh flow of air) and as much humidity as possible. Use trays of gravel; set potted plants on the moist gravel.

Feeding: Feed every other watering as long as light is good, and turn the plants so all parts have ample light.

Note: Watch for mealybugs and red spider on plants and if they attack follow directions in Chapter 5.

BROMELIADS

At this season most bromeliads will be growing, and some will be coming into bloom. At bloom time or shortly thereafter most bromeliads "throw" offshoots — new plants — because after a bromeliad blooms, it dies. The offshoots will supply new plants. Root them in starting mix.

Water and Light: While the potting medium should be somewhat dry, the "vases" of the plants should be filled with water. Plants can take sunlight now to mature growth and to encourage flowering. If you moved them to bright light in spring as recommended, now you can put them in sun. Provide good ventilation; this is vital in summer when it can get very hot indoors. Be sure windows are open and there is a good flow of air.

Temperature and Humidity: The warmth of summer will be beneficial for bromeliads; however, mist plants frequently to maintain good humidity and wipe leaves occasionally with a damp cloth to keep them shiny.

Feeding: While it is tempting to feed plants now to force them into growth, do not do it. Allow them to grow on their own.

BULBS

Bulbs that grow all year may be starting into flower now or may be ending their growing cycle. Treat the bulbous plants you have now as standard house plants.

Water and Light: Keep soil evenly moist. Be sure excess water does not accumulate in soil; drainage must be perfect for bulbs. Bulbs that are still growing need a bright place; those that have finished flowering should be stored in a cool dry place with only scant watering and little or no light.

Temperature and Humidity: Try to keep bulbous plants as cool as possible and keep them where there is good air circulation.

CACTI

This is the season when many cacti will be blooming. Since most are small plants they are ideally suited to windowsills, where their beautiful flowers provide a lovely scene.

Water and Light: Water cacti heavily and then allow them to dry out somewhat between waterings; these plants take summer heat and sun, so place them in the brightest windows for maximum bloom.

Temperature and Humidity: Warmth (80°F plus) is beneficial for most cacti, so don't worry about very hot days. It is, however, advisable to provide good air circulation and humidity. While many plants enjoy misting in summer, cacti do not; in fact, try to avoid getting water on the plants as rot may develop. To provide humidity, set them on damp gravel.

Feeding: I rarely feed cacti but if your plants have been in the same soil for more than a year, a weak fertilizer such as 10-10-5 applied about once a month is beneficial.

Note: Inspect plants occasionally for insects; mealybugs have a fondness for cacti and once they get a foothold they are difficult to eliminate. If they are caught early, the old-fashioned remedies mentioned in Chapter 5 eliminate them.

FERNS

Ferns will grow rapidly during this time of year, so be prepared to give them some extra attention. Since a well-grown fern is a prize indeed, the extra attention is worth it.

Water and Light: Keep soil evenly moist and spray plants with water to provide additional humidity during these hot months. Remember, ferns are shade denizens and extreme heat and dryness can quickly desiccate them. Keep them out of sun; these are fine plants for the north and west windows.

Temperature and Humidity: Provide a cool (68°F) location for plants. Ferns don't like extreme heat and, as noted above, should be protected from bright sun. Increase humidity by spraying water or using a small space humidifier.

Feeding: Use some fish emulsion for ferns now as you did in spring, applying it about once a month. Avoid standard plant foods; they generally cause fern fronds to turn brown at the tips.

Note: Sometimes ferns can be attacked by red spider so keep a watchful eye for streaked leaves or webs; use preventatives mentioned in Chapter 5.

FOLIAGE PLANTS

During the summer use the same care schedule outlined for spring.

Water and Light: Keep soil evenly moist. Be sure that plants have good bright light; sun is not necessary. Wipe leaves with a damp cloth and do not pamper plants. More foliage plants are killed by over-watering during this time of year than by any other cause.

Temperature and Humidity: There is really no special consideration necessary; try to keep plants as cool as possible (70°F) during the hot days and maintain good humidity (30 percent).

Feeding: Continue to feed plants once a month, as they make fast growth now. Also at this time add some fish emulsion; follow directions on package.

FLOWERING PLANTS

Now many flowering plants bear beautiful flowers to brighten the summer days. And many keep blooming, one flower following another, for several weeks.

Water and Light: Keep plants quite moist; the soil should be almost wet but never soggy. In many cases you might have to water plants three times a week, but of course this will depend on the size of the pot, whether it is clay or plastic, and specific indoor conditions. Give plants as much sun as possible; put them in south or east windows.

Temperature and Humidity: Average home temperatures of 75°F are fine. Mist plants frequently, especially when they are in bud, so flowers can open. Too much dry air causes buds to drop.

Feeding: Continue feeding once a month.

GERANIUMS

Many geraniums are now in beautiful flower and blaze with color in shades of red, orange, pink, or white, making lovely indoor accents. Consider yourself fortunate if you have amassed a healthy collection of geraniums.

Water and Light: Keep soil evenly moist, never dry, never soggy. It is far better to underwater plants than overwater them since many of them have semisucculent stems and can store some water. Move plants out of direct sun into bright light. Intense sun may scorch them.

Temperature and Humidity: Keep plants as cool as possible and do not subject them to high humidity even in the hot season.

Feeding: Feed moderately about every fourth or fifth watering with a 10-10-5 fertilizer.

GESNERIADS

Summer is peak blooming time for aeschynanthus, kohlerias, and columneas, and prettier flowers are hard to find. Even without flowers you will find that most gesneriads are handsome because of their foliage; especially episcias with their tapestry-colored leaves.

Water and Light: Water plants heavily now; soil should be evenly moist. Place plants in light but out of intense sun.

Temperature and Humidity: Keep a buoyant atmosphere and mist plants occasionally to maintain good humidity.

Feeding: Feed plants at least once a month; growth should be lush. Again, use a 10-10-5 fertilizer for maximum results.

Note: Insects have a fondness for these plants, so be on the watch for mealybugs and aphids especially. Use preventative methods outlined in Chapter 5.

ORCHIDS

Orchids do not like extreme heat; indeed more are killed from excessive heat and sun than any other cause. Thus it is imperative that you keep the plants as cool as possible at this time of year.

Water and Light: In the hot months orchids need even moisture; keep growing medium uniformly moist. Mist plants with tepid water as often as possible to cool the plants and at the same time help increase humidity. Keep orchids in bright places; most orchids will appreciate the light. However, watch to see if the light is too much for them. If you see brown or black areas developing on leaves, the sun is too hot for the plants; move them to another area.

Temperature and Humidity: As in spring, keep humidity at a good level by misting plants; a small space humidifier can be used to furnish additional moisture in the air. Again, keep ventilation at a maximum; a fresh flow of air is beneficial to these plants.

Feeding: If you are tempted to feed orchids, don't do it. Remember the spring admonition: too much feeding can kill orchids. These are really creatures of nature; let them grow on their own.

PALMS

Palms lend their tropical character to your home especially well now. Use them in room corners, in a garden room (if you have one), anywhere where you want lush green accents.

Water and Light: Keep plants well watered at this time of year; flood them every third day. Most palms are in large pots of 10 to 12 inches; those in smaller pots need even more water. Good light is essential now as plants make fast growth, but sunlight is not necessary.

Temperature and Humidity: Palms like heat, so don't worry about dog days. However, mist plants with tepid water occasionally to help increase humidity.

Feeding: Use some plant food now but not too much: one application of 10-10-5 every four weeks.

Note: Keep a lookout these hot months for insects on fronds; you can see the most common insects such as mealybugs and red spider mite. (See Chapter 5 on ways to get rid of bugs.)

SUCCULENTS

With warm weather succulents reach peak form, making handsome additions to the indoor garden. Crassulas and echeverias are especially good house plants.

Water and Light: Keep soil evenly moist and be sure pots have drainage facilities so excess water escapes. Succulents do not tolerate a saturated soil. With sunlight intense now, move plants out of direct rays; bright light is fine. Like orchids, succulent leaves may be scorched by intense sun.

Temperature and Humidity: Summer heat generally does not harm succulents as long as there is good air circulation. While some plants need high humidity now, succulents can tolerate low humidity if necessary; however, optimum humidity would be about 30 percent.

Feeding: During this season apply fish emulsion to plants once a month but try to avoid other supplemental food. Accumulated salts from plant food can become locked in the soil and harm succulents.

HOUSE PLANTS FOR SUMMER

ACALYPHA GODSEFFIANA
A showy plant, to 20 inches, with bright-green yellow-edged leaves. It needs sun and an evenly moist soil; plant bears unusual green-white flowers.
Fall: Follow spring schedule.
Winter: Follow spring schedule.
Spring: Water heavily. Sun.

ACALYPHA WILKESIANA
This colorful beauty grows to 30 inches with bronze and copper foliage and red blooms. Provide good sun and keep the soil evenly moist. An unusual plant.
Fall: Follow spring schedule.
Winter: Follow spring schedule.
Spring: Water heavily. Sun.

ACANTHUS MONTANUS   Grecian urn plant
To 60 inches, acanthus is a decorative treelike plant with large black-green leaves. Even indoors at a bright window it bears spikes of whitish-pink flowers on tall stalks. Grow the plant quite wet. This is basically an outdoor plant but it does well indoors.
Fall: Follow summer schedule.
Winter: Keep soil barely moist. Sun.
Spring: Increase waterings. Sun.

ACHIMENES GRANDIFLORA   rainbow flower
This plant is a beautiful summer display; it grows to 20 inches and produces purple flowers with white throats. Blooms continue for about two months. Start achimenes tubers, using six or seven to a 6-inch pot, any time from January on. Give tubers plenty of heat (80° F) and water. When flowers fade, store pots in a shady cool place (60° F) and in very early spring repot the tubers in fresh soil. See Chapter 7 for more information.

ACHIMENES LONGIFLORA   rainbow flower
A beautiful bower of flowers makes *A. longiflora* worth space at any window. Like other achimenes it grows from a small bulb. Use six or seven to a 6-inch pot and treat the same as *A. grandiflora*. See Chapter 7 for more information.

ACINETA DENSA
This orchid grows to 24 inches and produces spectacular flowers in mid-August. The blooms — yellow with red spots — appear on a pendent scape, so use open slatted baskets for acineta. Give the plant a few hours of morning sun and keep the potting mix evenly moist but never wet. This is a difficult plant to get to bloom, but its beauty makes it worth trying.
Fall: Reduce watering. Low light.
Winter: Keep evenly moist. Bright light.
Spring: Increase moisture. Keep out of sun. Low light.

AESCHYNANTHUS LOBBIANUS
Summer-flowering, these 30-inch plants are not the easiest to grow but the brilliant red flowers are worth the effort. The plant is a trailer and requires a rather bright, but not sunny, moist place. In active growth aeschynanthus needs plenty of water.
Fall: Keep evenly moist. Low light.
Winter: Keep evenly moist. Sun.
Spring: Increase waterings. Bright light.

Acalypha godseffiana

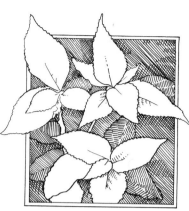

Acalypha wilkesiana

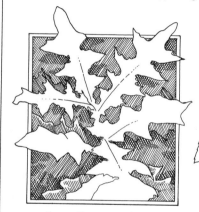

Acanthus montanus

Achimenes grandiflora

Achimenes longiflora

Acineta densa

Aeschynanthus lobbianus

AESCHYNANTHUS SPECIOSUS
lipstick vine

A very popular trailing plant, to 36 inches, that bears fine orange-red flowers in midsummer; the plant in full bloom is striking. Lipstick vines require a bright place and good moisture while growing. Excellent for baskets.

Fall: Keep evenly moist. Bright light.
Winter: Keep evenly moist. Sun.
Spring: Increase waterings. Bright light only.

AGAPANTHUS AFRICANUS
lily-of-the-Nile

An absolutely charming plant that *does bloom indoors* and is quite a beauty. Buy started plants from nurseries. With straplike leaves, and growing to 36 inches, the plant bears clusters of lovely blue flowers around June. Keep plant potbound and in a bright window. Water freely; after it flowers carry somewhat dry through late summer. When foliage dies down, store plant in basement or garage at 40 to 50° F and water once a month until it is time to start the plant again.
See Chapter 7 for more information.

ALOCASIA AMAZONICA

A stunning foliage plant, alocasia grows to 20 inches, with large dark-green leaves beautifully veined with ivory white. Keep in a bright but never sunny place; soil must be evenly moist, never too dry or too wet. Be sure the plant gets good humidity, at least 40 percent.

All Year: Follow summer schedule.

ALOCASIA CUPREA

A small plant, to 14 inches, with shiny purple foliage, *A. cuprea* adds fine color indoors. It needs an evenly moist soil and is somewhat easier to grow than most alocasias. Place in bright light, never sun.

All Year: Follow summer schedule.

ALOCASIA LOWI-GRANDIS

Probably the most popular alocasia, this one grows to 30 inches and has large metallic brown-green leaves. It needs moderate or low light with good moisture.

All Year: Follow summer schedule.

ALSTROEMERIA PULCHELLA

This amaryllis is at its peak in summer with green flowers spotted brown and tipped red. Get this plant at a nursery and pot it in a loose humusy soil in a 6-inch container. Water sparingly and bring into growth slowly; shade it through the summer. After foliage dies in fall, keep plants on the dry side until March and then repot in fresh soil.
See Chapter 7 for more information.

ANANAS COSMOSUS
pineapple plant

First, do not expect pineapples from your plant; you will not get them, but you will get a lovely rosette type of bromeliad with 20-inch dark-green leaves. Use an equal mixture of soil and fine fir bark kept evenly moist, and grow in bright light. Indestructible bromeliad.

Fall: Keep evenly moist. Sun.
Winter: Keep evenly moist. Sun.
Spring: Increase waterings. Sun.

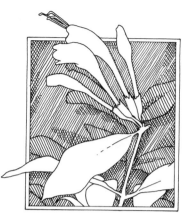

Aeschynanthus speciosus

Agapanthus africanus

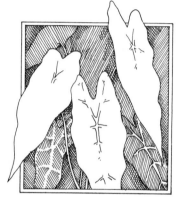

Alocasia amazonica

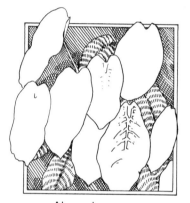

Alocasia cuprea

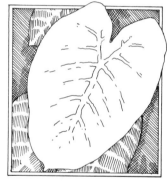

Alocasia lowi-grandis

Alstroemeria pulchella

Ananas cosmosus

ANANAS NANA
miniature pineapple

This lovely pineapple looks like *A. cosmosus* but only grows to about 14 inches. It requires little care other than bright light and even moisture. Excellent under artificial light.

Fall: Keep evenly moist. Sun.
Winter: Keep evenly moist. Sun.
Spring: Increase waterings. Sun.

ANSELLIA GIGANTEA
spider orchid

If you want a dependable orchid to bloom every summer, this is it. It grows to 30 inches and produces small pretty flowers spotted red. The plant requires abundant moisture and sun. Get plants from orchid suppliers.

All Year: Follow summer schedule.

APHELANDRA CHAMAISSIONA
zebra plant

A 14-inch popular house plant with gray-green leaves and an unusual spike of yellow flowers in midsummer. Not easy to grow, *A. chamaissiona* needs a bright place and evenly moist soil.

Fall: Follow summer schedule. Sun.
Winter: Dry out between waterings. Sun.
Spring: Keep soil evenly moist. Bright light.

APHELANDRA ROEZLII

This aphelandra is a better plant than *A. chamaissiona*. It grows to 16 inches, is more robust, and bears a stunning red flower spike. Keep plant in bright light and water it rather heavily.

Fall: Follow summer schedule. Sun.
Winter: Dry out between waterings. Sun.
Spring: Keep soil evenly moist. Bright light.

BEAUCARNEA RECURVATA
pony tail

This plant appears bizarre to some, beautiful to others. From the lily family, it grows about 20 inches tall and has a bulbous base and curving grassy leaves. The plant needs good light and is fairly undemanding.

Fall: Follow summer schedule. Sun.
Winter: Dry out between waterings. Sun.
Spring: Keep evenly moist. Sun.

BELOPERONE GUTTATA
shrimp plant

An old-fashioned plant, this one grows to 30 inches. It is bushy, with bright-green leaves and coral-colored bracts that somehow resemble small shrimp. Needs sun; allow to dry out between waterings. Prune back leggy growth in late summer to encourage fresh shoots.

Fall: Keep soil evenly moist. Sun.
Winter: Dry out between waterings. Sun.
Spring: Provide ample water. Bright light.

BROUGHTONIA SANGUINEA

This miniature 6-inch orchid bears small cerise flowers from autumn to winter. Good for the beginner because it is so easy to grow. Give it bright sun and plenty of water.

Fall: Keep evenly moist. Sun.
Winter: Dry out between waterings. Sun.
Spring: Provide ample water. Sun.

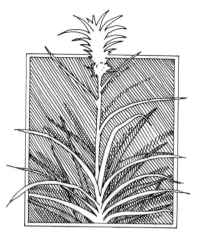

Ananas nana

Ansellia gigantea

Aphelandra chamaissiona

Aphelandra roezlii

Beaucarnea recurvata

Beloperone guttata

Broughtonia sanguinea

BROWALLIA SPECIOSA
This outdoor annual makes a fine indoor plant, growing to about 24 inches and bearing fine blue flowers for several weeks. It requires ample sun and good moisture; blooms only in summer.

CALADIUM 'JUNE BRIDE'
Caladiums grow to 30 inches, with paper-thin, heart-shaped leaves; many color combinations available. Provide low light and warmth, and water well in growth; they like it wet. At the end of fall when leaves die down, reduce amount of water and remove tubers from pots; store them in brown paper sacks at 60° F for two to three months. Then repot, one tuber to a 5-inch container.
See Chapter 7 for more information.

CLERODENDRUM THOMSONIAE   glory bower
Overlooked by indoor gardeners for some time, these rather large 48-inch vining plants have red and white flowers. Plants need some sun, and you should keep soil evenly moist. Very decorative as summer pot plants.
Fall: Keep evenly moist. Sun.
Winter: Dry out between waterings. Sun.
Spring: Increase moisture. Bright light.

COBEA SCANDENS   cup-and-saucer vine
A charming 60-inch vine with fine purple flowers that bloom on and off through summer. Sow some seed in May or June in a clay pot and start watering; when plants start growing put in sun and keep soil very moist. An amenable plant, good only for one season but worth its modest price.

CODIAEUM VARIEGATUM PICTUM   croton
These exciting foliage plants grow to about 36 inches. They have leaves in colors that run from pink to yellow to orange, red, and brown and shades in between. Crotons need good sun and lots of water, as well as ample air circulation. Only in winter can you allow plants to rest with scant waterings.
Fall: Keep evenly moist. Sun.
Winter: Dry out between waterings. Sun.
Spring: Keep evenly moist. Sun.

COELOGYNE OCHRACEA
A rather small 14-inch orchid with orange and white flowers. The plant prefers coolness and some sun and even moisture until bloom. After flowers fade, grow somewhat dry for about two months. Pot in fine-grade fir bark.
Fall: Dry out slightly. Sun.
Winter: Keep evenly moist. Sun.
Spring: Dry out to encourage flower buds. Bright light.

COLEUS BLUMEI
Now available in many varieties, coleus plants are old-fashioned favorites with multicolored large heart-shaped leaves. Plants grow to 18 inches and need buckets of water and plenty of bright light.
Fall: Keep evenly moist. Bright light.
Winter: Dry out. Cut back to 6 inches; repot. Sun.
Spring: Increase waterings. Bright light.

Browallia speciosa

Caladium 'June Bride'

Clerodendrum thomsoniae

Cobea scandens

Codiaeum variegatum pictum

Coleus blumei

Coelogyne ochracea

COSTUS IGNEUS
spiral ginger

A handsome 30-inch plant with open-faced orange flowers. Give it a bright place and keep soil evenly moist. The flowers appear throughout summer, sometimes into fall.

Fall: Keep soil evenly moist. Bright light.
Winter: Dry out between waterings. Bright light.
Spring: Provide ample moisture. Bright light.

CRINUM MOOREI

Here is a 40-inch bulbous plant with pink blooms in summer. Plant in March, one bulb to a 2-inch pot, with the tip of bulb protruding just above the soil line. Water heavily *after growth starts.* Shade from hot sun but do provide good light. After plants flower, move to a shady place and water scantily for two months. Then resume moderate waterings and return to a bright window. See Chapter 7 for more information.

CRINUM POWELLI ALBA

This white-flowering crinum is just as nice as the other crinum described. It grows to about 36 inches and is treated in the same manner. See Chapter 7 for more information.

DIPLADENIA AMOENA
Mexican love vine

A fast-growing lovely vine, to 40 inches, with bright-green leaves and exquisite funnel-shaped pink flowers, dipladenia is a joy to the indoor gardener. It is a greedy plant that needs plenty of water and sun, but provides lots of color for very little effort.

Fall: Keep evenly moist. Sun.
Winter: Dry out between waterings. Sun.
Spring: Provide ample moisture. Sun.

ECHINOCACTUS GRUSONI
golden barrel

The golden barrel is a popular cactus, 12 to 14 inches in diameter and covered with long yellow spines. It needs bright light and moderate waterings. Do not expect flowers indoors.

Fall: Keep evenly moist. Sun.
Winter: Dry out between waterings. Sun essential.
Spring: Provide ample water. Sun.

ECHINOCACTUS INGENS

This is a huge brownish-blue cactus that can grow to 30 inches in diameter. Obviously, it can only be for a special place (and those with space for it). Like most cacti it needs moderate watering and a bright place. Only for the brave (spines are vicious).

Fall: Keep evenly moist. Sun.
Winter: Keep barely moist. Sun essential; also coolness.
Spring: Provide ample moisture. Sun.

ECHINOCEREUS BALEYII

This miniature cactus, to 4 inches, is cylindrical in growth and bears pretty pink flowers. It needs some sunlight and moderate watering, and is an undemanding plant you never need fear will die.

Fall: Keep evenly moist. Sun.
Winter: Keep barely moist. Coolness essential (60° F). Sun.
Spring: Provide ample moisture. Sun.

Costus igneus

Crinum moorie

Crinum powelli alba

Dipladenia amoena

Echinocactus grusoni

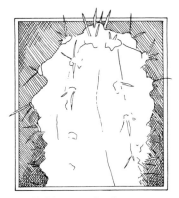

Echinocactus ingens

Echinocereus baleyii

ECHINOCEREUS REICHENBACHII   lace cactus
Another fine plant, this globe-shaped cactus grows to 12 inches, and bears
white to red-brown flowers. It needs some sun and moderate waterings.
Fall: Keep evenly moist. Sun.
Winter: Keep barely moist. Sun.
Spring: Provide ample watering. Sun.

EPIPHYLLUM   orchid cactus
Unlike desert cactus, epiphyllums are tree dwellers in cool moist rain forests.
To 20 inches, they bear stellar large flowers in many colors; although blooms
last only a few days the plants are desirable. Give epiphyllums bright sun and
an evenly moist soil. Most bloom freely in mid or late summer.
Fall: Keep evenly moist. Bright light.
Winter: Keep barely moist. Bright light.
Spring: Increase waterings. Sun.

EPISCIA CUPREATA
This is a fine gesneriad with copper foliage and red flowers. It grows to
about 20 inches and blooms in summer. Give episcia plenty of water, keep
the soil evenly moist, and place it in a bright but not sunny place.
Fall: Dry out between waterings. Sun.
Winter: Dry out between waterings. Sun.
Spring: Increase moisture. Bright light only.

EPISCIA LILACINA
This episcia has coppery foliage and lavender flowers in summer. Growing to
20 inches, the plant needs bright light and plenty of water. Can be used as a
hanging basket plant. Good for artificial light gardens.
Fall: Dry out between waterings. Sun.
Winter: Dry out between waterings. Sun.
Spring: Increase moisture. Bright light only.

EUCOMIS PUNCTATA   pineapple lily
A bulbous plant, to 40 inches, eucomis has dark-green foliage and handsome
crowns of small greenish-white flowers in July or August. The plant needs
bright light. Allow soil to dry out between waterings. In spring, plant one bulb
to a 6-inch pot with top of bulb protruding slightly above the soil line. Start into
growth with scanty watering and increase as foliage matures. Do not store;
eucomis grows all year long. See Chapter 7 for more information.

FUCHSIA   lady's eardrops
Outdoors these magnificent flowering plants decorate many patios. Indoors, if
you have perseverance, you might be able to get them to bear some flowers.
The problem is that these pendent growers need cool nights (60° F), and in hot
summers this is almost impossible to achieve. Fuchsias require buckets of
water and need to be cut back to 4 inches after flowering in fall. Allow a dry
rest and then resume watering in spring to get fresh new growth.

GARDENIA JASMINOIDES   Cape jasmine
Though loved by many, the gardenia is also hated by many because it drops
buds just when it is ready to bloom in summer. The trick is to mist the buds
and protect the plant from drafts or fluctuating temperatures. Gardenias grow
to about 40 inches, with scented waxy white flowers. Provide plenty of water
and sun; then, after bloom, grow on the dry side in a bright place.
Fall: Keep evenly moist. Sun.
Winter: Keep evenly moist. Provide ample humidity. Sun.
Spring: Dry out between waterings. Provide ample humidity. Sun.

Echinocereus reichenbachii

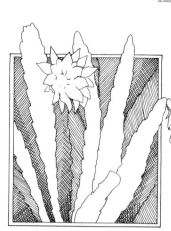

Epiphyllum

Episcia cupreata

Episcia lilacina

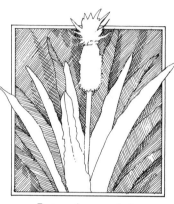

Eucomis punctata

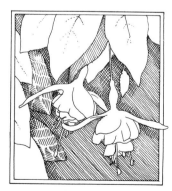

Fuchsia

Gardenia jasminoides

GLORIOSA ROTHSCHILDIANA · glory lily

This is a popular 40-inch vining plant with exquisite orange lilylike flowers. The plant is grown from a bulb started in spring or summer, one to a 7-inch pot. Give bright light once the leaves are growing; keep soil evenly moist. Rest for three months and start again in late fall. See Chapter 7 for further information.

GLOXINIA

A popular gift plant, gloxinias grow to 20 inches and produce mammoth flowers — blue, red, pink — a tremendous summer display. Your plant will probably come from the florist or nursery. Treat it gently the first few weeks by giving it as much coolness as possible. Keep it out of direct sun, and when blooming is over, store the bulb in its container in a dry, shady, cool place. Start the gloxinia again in late fall by repotting it in fresh soil. See Chapter 7 for more information.

HIPPEASTRUM · amaryllis

This popular gift plant bears tremendous 7-inch flowers that may be red or white or multicolored. Plants grow to 40 inches. Bulbs are started from December to March using one bulb to a 7-inch pot. Don't bury the bulb; let the upper third reach above the soil line. Set the pot in a cool dark place and grow almost dry until the bud is up about 6 inches. Then move into sun and water heavily. After blooming the plant should be kept growing so leaves can manufacture food for spring flowering. See Chapter 7 for more information.

HOYA BELLA · miniature wax plant

This wax plant is not as popular as *H. carnosa* and it is tougher to grow. Its advantage is its size, which rarely exceeds 16 inches. Yet it is difficult to coax into bloom. Give it even moisture and good sun and hope for the best.

Fall: Keep evenly moist. Sun.
Winter: Dry out between waterings. Sun.
Spring: Keep evenly moist. Sun.

HOYA CARNOSA · wax plant

A favorite, the wax plant is a splendid vining 30-inch plant with leathery leaves and clusters of very fragrant waxy white and pink flowers that are delightful in midsummer. Only mature 4 to 5-year-old plants will bloom; they need full sun to form buds. Grow potbound and give plenty of water. Don't remove stem or spur on which flowers are produced; this is the source of next season's blooms.

Fall: Keep evenly moist. Sun.
Winter: Dry out severely between waterings. Sun.
Spring: Keep evenly moist. Sun.

HYPOESTES SANGUINOLENTA · polka-dot plant

Hypoestes is a small 10-inch plant good for terrarium gardening as well as the windowsill. It has small round leaves dotted yellow, and grows in a branching habit. It needs good moisture and bright light.

All Year: Follow summer schedule.

IMPATIENS

For late summer bloom, the new varieties of impatiens are excellent. These 20-inch plants bear dark-green leaves and bright red or pink flowers that brighten any area. The plants need evenly moist soil — never let them dry out — and bright but not sunny light. Impatiens are at nurseries, and while they are only good for the season, from about July to September, they are well worth the money.

Gloriosa rothschildiana

Gloxinia

Hippeastrum

Hoya bella

Hoya carnosa

Hypoestes sanguinolenta

Impatiens

JATROPHA PANDURIFOLIA

A tropical evergreen shrub growing to 40 inches, jatropha with its broad green leaves and red flowers is lovely. It needs sunlight; let soil dry out between waterings. Flowers appear on and off throughout summer and well into fall.

Fall: Keep evenly moist. Sun.
Winter: Dry out between waterings. Sun.
Spring: Provide plenty of water. Sun.

KAEMPFERA ROSCOEANA   peacock plant

If you want a compact bushy plant with exquisite foliage, the peacock plant is your answer. It has beautiful blue-green, almost iridescent leaves and lavender flowers. The plant grows to 12 inches and needs bright light and an evenly moist soil. Let plant die down in winter.

Fall: Keep evenly moist. Sun.
Winter: Let dry out; store in a paper sack at 60° F.
Spring: Repot. Resume watering. Sun.

KOHLERIA AMABILIS

Growing to 16 inches, with green leaves and pink flowers, kohlerias are in color in summer. The plant needs bright light; water it heavily during growth. This is a pretty plant but somewhat difficult to grow. Good under lights.

Fall: Keep evenly moist. Bright light.
Winter: Keep evenly moist. Sun.
Spring: Provide ample water. Bright light.

KOHLERIA ERINTHINA

Another excellent kohleria, this one is an upright grower to 24 inches, with brilliant red flowers in summer. It needs bright light and plenty of water during growth.

Fall: Keep evenly moist. Bright light.
Winter: Keep evenly moist. Sun.
Spring: Provide ample water. Bright light.

LOCKHARTIA OERSTEDII   chain orchid

Hardly looking like an orchid, lockhartia has tiny dark-green leaves that grow in chain fashion. The plant is about 16 inches tall and has tiny yellow flowers on and off in July and August. Lockhartia needs an evenly moist medium and bright sun. Plant in fine-grade fir bark.

All Year: Follow summer schedule.

MAMMILLARIA BOCASANA   pincushion cactus

A very fine cactus, to 20 inches in diameter, mammillaria has colorful spines and tiny white flowers in summer. This desert plant is easily grown in sun with even moisture.

Fall: Keep evenly moist. Sun.
Winter: Keep barely moist. Sun.
Spring: Provide ample water. Sun.

MAMMILLARIA ELONGATA

Not as ornamental as *M. bocasana,* this cactus is a 14-inch globe and bears white flowers in summer. It needs an evenly moist soil. Give bright light.

Fall: Keep evenly moist. Sun.
Winter: Keep barely moist. Sun.
Spring: Provide ample water. Sun.

Jatropha pandurifolia

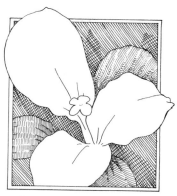

Kaempfera roscoeana

Kohleria amabilis

Kohleria erinthina

Lockhartia oerstedii

Mammillaria bocasana

Mammillaria elongata

NERIUM OLEANDER
oleander

A leafy plant, to 40 inches, bearing white or pink flowers, oleander needs buckets of water, sun, and occasional pruning to keep it in bounds. While it is not spectacular, it produces flowers annually in summer. A good one for beginners.

Fall: Needs plenty of water. Sun.
Winter: Keep evenly moist. Sun.
Spring: Needs plenty of water. Sun.

PANDANUS UTILIS

Not as pretty as *P. veitchii*, and growing to 40 inches in diameter, this one has olive-green leaves. Give it an evenly moist soil and bright light and it takes care of itself.

All Year: Follow summer schedule.

PANDANUS VEITCHII
screw pine

A good all-around house plant, pandanus has a rosette shape, to 40 inches, and lovely white and green straplike leaves. Plants need some bright light (but no sun) and an evenly moist soil. This is a plant that is almost impossible to kill.

All Year: Follow summer schedule.

PELARGONIUM 'PRINCE RUPERT'

'Prince Rupert' is a rangy geranium growing to about 20 inches; it has yellow and green leaves. It requires little care other than an evenly moist soil and bright light.

Fall: Keep evenly moist. Bright light.
Winter: Keep evenly moist. Sun.
Spring: Cut back to 6 inches; repot. Provide ample water. Sun.

PHILODENDRON 'BURGUNDY'

From the large philodendron family, *P.* 'Burgundy' with its blood-wine leaves grows to 30 inches. Like most philodendrons it requires an evenly moist soil. It is a vine so needs some support — a totem pole or trellis — to grow well. Keep it in moderate or low light. One of the better varieties.

Fall: Keep evenly moist. Moderate light.
Winter: Keep barely moist. Some sun.
Spring: Provide ample water. Moderate light.

PHILODENDRON HASTATUM

A popular philodendron with lance-shaped leaves; grows to 30 inches and is relatively easy to grow. Give it moderate or low light and keep soil evenly moist. This is a semiviner that will need support, so use a pole or trellis in the soil.

Fall: Keep evenly moist. Moderate light.
Winter: Dry out between waterings; move to coolness (60° F).
Spring: Provide ample water and more warmth. Moderate light.

PHILODENDRON PANDURAEFORME
fiddleleaf philodendron

With exquisite scalloped leaves, *P. panduraeforme* grows to 40 inches. The dark-green foliage of this vine makes it a fine room plant. It needs a bright but not sunny place and an evenly moist soil.

Fall: Follow summer schedule. Moderate light.
Winter: Dry out between waterings. Some sun.
Spring: Keep evenly moist. Moderate light.

Nerium oleander

Pandanus veitchii

Pandanus utilis

Pelargonium 'Prince Rupert'

Philodendron 'Burgundy'

Philodendron hastatum

Philodendron panduraeforme

PHILODENDRON SELLOUM
With lobed leaves and rosette growth, *P. selloum* grows to 30 inches. It needs moderate light and an evenly moist soil; easy to grow. It can get straggly, so prune back occasionally to encourage bushiness.
All Year: Follow summer schedule.

PHILODENDRON WENDLANDII
This is a self-heading philodendron that grows in cabbage habit and makes a spectacular 30-inch plant. The leaves are broad, spatula-shaped, and shiny green. Grow it in bright light and allow soil to dry out between waterings.
Fall: Keep evenly moist. Bright light.
Winter: Dry out between waterings. Bright light.
Spring: Provide ample water. Bright light.

PILEA CADIERII   aluminum plant
Sometimes called watermelon pilea, this pilea grows to 12 inches and has silver and green foliage. It requires little care, a bright location, and ample watering. A good dependable plant, excellent for dish garden or terrarium.
All Year: Follow summer schedule.

PILEA INVOLUCRATA
Here is a pilea known for its bushy growth and brown leaves; it grows to 14 inches. Like most pileas it requires minimum care: ample water and a bright location. Fine for dish gardens and terrariums.
All Year: Follow summer schedule.

PLECTRANTHUS AUSTRALIS   Swedish ivy
This is a foolproof plant with waxy green leaves on trailing stems to 20 inches. Pink flowers sometimes appear in late summer. Grow in moderate or low light and keep soil evenly moist. Fine basket plant.
All Year: Follow summer schedule.

PLECTRANTHUS OERTENDAHII   Swedish ivy
This easy basket plant, also called Swedish ivy, grows to 30 inches. It has bright-green scalloped leaves and it grows fast. *P. oertendahii* needs moderate light and should be allowed to dry out between waterings.
All Year: Follow summer schedule.

PLEOMELE ANGUSTIFOLIA
With dark-green narrow leaves, growing to 24 inches, pleomele has a compact habit. It needs ample moisture and moderate or low light. Grow several to a pot for a good display. Another easy plant to grow.
Fall: Keep evenly moist. Moderate light.
Winter: Dry out somewhat between waterings. Sun.
Spring: Keep evenly moist. Moderate light.

Philodendron selloum

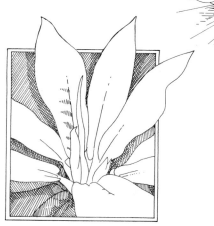

Philodendron wendlandii

Pilea cadierii

Pilea involucrata

Plectranthus australis

Plectranthus oertendahii

Pleomele angustifolia

PLUMBAGO CAPENSIS
leadwort

This 36-inch shrub has small leaves and cheerful blue flowers in August. It is a sprawling plant that climbs or trails and every year should be cut back somewhat to encourage fresh growth. Grow plumbago in sun; keep very moist during the warm months. A large plant for room accent.

Fall: Keep evenly moist. Sun.
Winter: Cut back to 10 inches; water scantily. Sun.
Spring: Resume watering. Sun.

RECHSTEINERIA LEUCOTRICHA
Brazilian edelweiss

A fine velvety-leaved 16-inch plant that bears tubular red flowers in summer, this is a member of the gesneriad family. Give rechsteineria more light than African violets but don't grow it in strong sun. Water moderately and after the plant blooms store in a dry, cool (60° F) place until late fall. Then start over again using fresh soil. Good under artificial light.
See Chapter 7 for more information.

RUSELLIA EQUISETIFORMIS
coral plant

Rusellia produces coral flowers on and off through the warm months and into fall. It is a 30-inch plant with oval leaves and is easy to grow. Give it ample moisture and sunshine.

Fall: Keep evenly moist. Sun.
Winter: Keep evenly moist. Sun.
Spring: Provide ample water. Bright light.

SANSEVIERIA EHRENBERGII

Growing in a fan fashion to 18 inches, this plant has blue-green leaves edged white. It is a tough plant that can take abuse if necessary. For optimum growth, give it moderate light and allow soil to dry out between waterings.
All Year: Follow summer schedule.

SANSEVIERIA TRIFASCIATA
snake plant

This is the indestructible snake plant that grows to 30 inches. It has lance-shaped green leaves banded with yellow and needs little attention other than moderate or low light and a somewhat dry soil.
All Year: Follow summer schedule.

SCHIZOCENTRON ELEGANS
Spanish shawl

This beauty is just right for a sunny cool window. The plant grows to 10 inches, with tiny leaves and fine cerise flowers in summer. Keep soil evenly moist; hard to find but worth the search.

Fall: Keep soil evenly moist. Sun.
Winter: Dry out somewhat between waterings. Sun.
Spring: Keep evenly moist. Bright light.

SCINDAPSUS AUREUS
ivy arum

This is a climber, to 24 inches, with smooth dark-green leaves splashed with yellow. Scindapsus grows lushly in moderate light with plenty of water. Good for baskets; nice in dish gardens too. There are several splendid varieties.
All Year: Follow summer schedule.

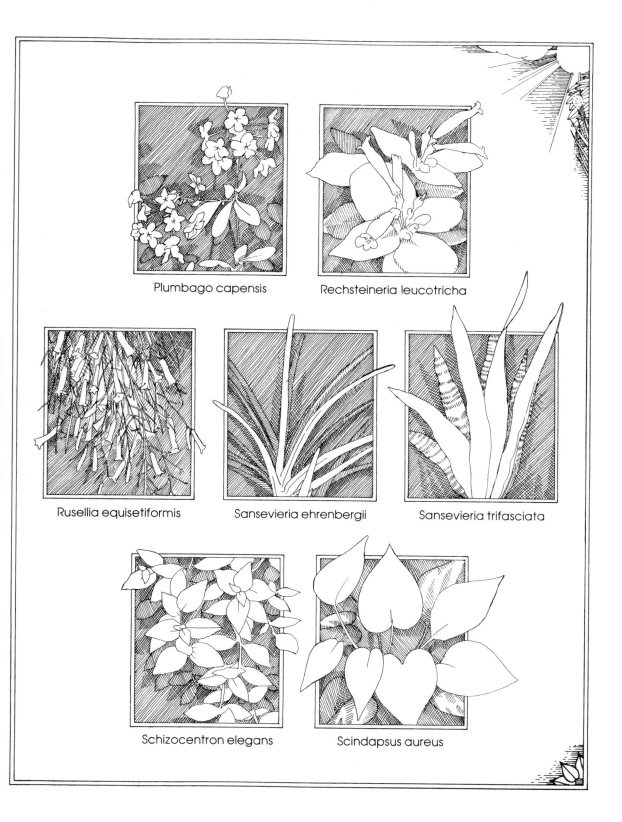

Plumbago capensis

Rechsteineria leucotricha

Rusellia equisetiformis

Sansevieria ehrenbergii

Sansevieria trifasciata

Schizocentron elegans

Scindapsus aureus

SEDUM MORGANIANUM
burro's tail

A succulent trailer, to 30 inches, with gray apple-green leaves. This plant needs pampering to grow well. Mainly, do not overwater it. Give it moderate light and good air circulation. Strictly a basket plant.

Fall: Keep evenly moist. Sun.
Winter: Keep barely moist. Sun.
Spring: Increase waterings. Bright light.

STANHOPEA OCULATA
cow's-horn orchid

A splendid 30-inch orchid with dark-green broad leaves and bizarre yellow and white flowers in August. Plants need even moisture and good sun. The flower spike grows from the bottom of the plant so use a slatted basket for it. grow in large-grade fir bark.

Fall: Give plenty of water. Sun.
Winter: Dry out somewhat. Sun.
Spring: Keep evenly moist. Bright light.

SYNGONIUM PODOPHYLLUM
arrowhead plant

This is a fast-growing 30-inch plant with lance-shaped leaves of white and green. It can be grown in water or soil and needs only low or moderate light to keep it lush. One of the easiest plants to grow.

All Year: Follow summer schedule.

TOLMIEA MENZIESII
piggyback plant

A popular basket plant, tolmiea has lobed papery leaves and grows to 16 inches or more in diameter. While it is beautiful, it requires water almost every day in the hot months. It needs moderate light; sun has a tendency to bake it.

Fall: Give plenty of water. Moderate light.
Winter: Keep evenly moist. Sun.
Spring: Give plenty of water. Moderate light.

TRADESCANTIA ALBIFLORA

This fast-growing trailer has white and green leaves and grows to 36 inches. It grows in moderate or low light and needs ample watering all year. Trim back occasionally to encourage fresh growth. Grow in hanging containers.

Fall: Follow summer schedule.
Winter: Dry out somewhat. Bright light.
Spring: Follow summer schedule.

TRADESCANTIA BLOSSFELDIANA
wandering Jew

This tradescantia is the popular green-leaved type that grows quickly and. easily. Trailing, it can reach 40 inches or more. It requires ample watering and moderate or low light. Good basket plant.

Fall: Follow summer schedule.
Winter: Keep evenly moist. Moderate light.
Spring: Follow summer schedule.

TRADESCANTIA FLUMENSIS
wandering Jew

Probably the best known trandescantia, *T. flumensis* has green leaves and like the other tradescantias grows easily with ample moisture and moderate light. Fine for baskets.

Fall: Follow summer schedule.
Winter: Keep evenly moist. Moderate light.
Spring: Follow summer schedule.

Sedum morganianum

Stanhopea oculata

Syngonium podophyllum

Tolmiea menziesii

Tradescantia albiflora

Tradescantia blossfeldiana

Tradescantia flumensis

TULBAGHIA FRAGRANS
society garlic

A bulbous plant that grows to 20 inches and resembles agapanthus, this lily has fragrant pink flowers in summer. Put several corms in a 6-inch pot of sandy soil in spring and give plenty of water in summer. Keep in bright light. Blooms on and off through summer. Dry off, repot in fall.
See Chapter 7 for more information.

VRIESEA CARINATA

Growing to 18 inches, this bromeliad has pale-green leaves and a yellow and crimson sword-shaped flower head. Grow the plant evenly moist; keep "vase" filled with water. Bright light is needed.
All Year: Follow summer schedule.

VRIESEA SPLENDENS
flaming sword

Because of the swordlike orange flower head this bromeliad is very popular; the green foliage with mahogany stripes is also distinctive. It needs good light and an evenly moist growing medium; keep the "vase" of the plant filled with water.
All Year: Follow summer schedule.

ZANTEDESCHIA AETHIOPICA
calla lily

A fine small 12-inch plant with grassy foliage and pretty white flowers, the calla lily is started from a bulb in spring and bears blooms now. Put one bulb to a 5-inch pot and place in a bright cool location. Water moderately; when leaves appear, keep soil evenly moist and move to sun. After flowers fade, ripen off foliage naturally by decreasing watering. Then put the pot in a cool (60° F) shady place and withhold water until early fall. Repot and start again.
See Chapter 7 for more information.

ZANTEDESCHIA ELLIOTTIANA
golden calla

This is called the golden calla because it bears yellow flowers. It is somewhat taller than *Z. aethiopica* but grown in the same manner. Lovely for cut flowers.
See Chapter 7 for more information.

ZANTEDESCHIA REHMANNI
pink calla

Grows to 20 inches; a beautiful pink-flowering species grown in the same manner as the other zantedeschias.
See Chapter 7 for more information.

ZEBRINA PENDULA
wandering Jew

This plant has the same common name as tradescantia. It has oval pointed purple leaves with silver bands — very colorful. A fast-growing trailer to 36 inches, the wandering Jew is a mass of color in sun. A splendid plant.
Fall: Keep evenly moist. Sun.
Winter: Keep evenly moist. Sun.
Spring: Provide ample water. Bright light.

Tulbaghia fragrans

Vriesea carinata

Vriesea splendens

Zantedeschia aethiopica

Zantedeschia elliottiana

Zantedeschia rehmanni

Zebrina pendula

PART THREE

FALL

7 GET READY FOR FALL

FALL TEMPERATURES are unpredictable. The next three months may be unseasonably hot or unseasonably cold or both, and fluctuating temperatures are hard on indoor plants. As the days shorten, plants don't have as much light as they do in spring or summer to help them assimilate nutrients. Although it's not apparent, there's a general slowing-down of plant growth. Feeding must be administered carefully now so as not to force new growth. Plants should not be stimulated when they're starting into their winter rest. See the seasonal check lists for specific information on feeding.

Since plants simply can't grow quickly in autumn's short days, too much water is also bad, so favor staying on the dry side. Much of your watering schedule will depend on how much artificial heat you use in the fall; the more heat, the more the plants will dry out. Also watch to see how the plants are getting along. Have they reached maturity for the year and do they now need a rest? Be alert now as you tend them. Autumn is the one time of the year when you *must* be an excellent gardener to get the most from your plants.

Although repotting is most often done in spring, if necessary you can also transplant plants in fall, ideally in September or October. This is also a good time to clean and scrub all pots, and to make sure that the indoor garden area is attractive.

Autumn is the time of the year to take inventory of the plants you want to keep. Space is often at a premium in homes and apartments, so it's sometimes wise to discard some weak plants (and there are plants that just won't adapt) for better, more handsome plants.

START A TERRARIUM

Terrariums — little green worlds in containers — are beautiful all year but in late fall they have special value. The landscape may be bleak outside, but inside, terrariums glow with green. You can duplicate woodland, forest, or desert scenes to decorate a windowsill, desk, or table. And most closed terrariums never need water after the initial watering. Leaves give off water; this moisture accumulates on the inside of the terrarium and rolls down into the soil, and the cycle goes on and on. Thus, a terrarium supplies its own moisture.

There are hundreds of containers you can use for terrariums. Some are large and expensive, and others are more modest in price. The plastic domes are fine, but be sure the dome is large enough. Growing plants properly in terrariums depends on the right amount of space for the right amount of plants.

A leaded-glass terrarium overflows with green plants to bring a spot of nature indoors. This open terrarium is easy to plant and will need water about once a week under average conditions. (Photo by Matthew Barr)

A terrarium can be in a bowl or a vase, open or closed.

This stained-glass terrarium has colored glass on roof and base. (Photo by Matthew Barr)

A homemade wooden-framed terrarium houses several small plants—fern and acorus. This diminutive scene never needs water. (Photo by author)

Pileas reside in a cathedral-type terrarium, a lovely accent for any table or desk. (Photo by Matthew Barr)

Glass terrariums come in many shapes, sizes, and designs. Some cost as much as $400, but small glass vases and jardinières and bottles cost only a few dollars. You can even use glass bottles and jugs that vinegar or distilled water comes in.

To plant a terrarium, put in a layer of gravel, about ½ inch, and then add some charcoal chips. Insert a bed of 4 to 5 inches of rich soil. Make planting holes and put plants in place, firming the soil around the collar of the plant. Water lightly; do not drench plants. Terrariums have no drainage facilities, so watch closed terrariums carefully. If the glass shows an excessive amount of condensation, remove the top for a few hours so air can circulate inside the tiny garden. If you don't do this, plants may rot overnight.

Always keep terrariums out of the sun. In the sun the inside of the garden becomes so hot that the plants bake to death. The best place for a terrarium is in bright light, where some natural light is available but where sun does not strike the container.

There are true miniatures in many plant families. There are miniature gloxinias, African violets, begonias, and even orchids, as well as small plants like peperomias and ferns that never grow over 8 inches or so. These are the ideal plants for your gardens under glass. Most miniature or dwarf plants are designated as such in suppliers' catalogs. Many plant stores now have what are called terrarium plants, but you should ask whether they are true miniatures or seedlings of standard size plants, since these may grow too large in a few months.

Try to grow compatible plants like ferns and peperomias, which like somewhat moist, shady conditions, or small orchids and African violets, which need similar conditions. Here are some miniatures that are especially good for terrariums, and instructions on how to plant and grow them.

African Violets

Grow miniature African violets in 2 parts garden loam to 1 part each charcoal, sand, peat moss, and leaf mold. Plants must have a spongy humusy mix so the roots can breathe and excess water can drain through the soil. During the day, let air circulate within the container: Remove the top for 1 hour or so, or prop matchsticks under the rim of the lid. Give plants bright light but no sun, and watch gardens for signs of mildew or botrytis, evidenced by gray mold on plants. Dust plants with a fungicide (Captan or Zineb) if the disease starts. Try the following African violet varieties:

'Honeyette.' Double red-lavender flowers. Only 5 inches across.

'Minneapolis.' Double pink flowers; plain green leaves.

'Sweet Sixteen.' Double white flowers; scalloped spoon-shaped leaves.

'Tiny Bells.' Single dark-blue flowers; quilted dark-green leaves.

'Wendy.' Large blue flowers; quilted leaves.

'White Doll.' Tiny plant with fine white flowers; blooms when only 2 inches tall.

Begonias

In winter and early spring, when color is scarce, miniature begonias in the terrarium come to the rescue — they bear charming bowers of cascading flowers with little effort. Plants grow slowly, but once they're established in the container they give a harvest of bloom, even without sun. The begonia family is large. There are hairy-leaved (hirsute), angel-wing, and rhizomatous (with sculptural rhizomes) begonias; each group includes delightful miniatures.

Begonias love the warmth and humidity of closed containers and need a soil of equal parts garden soil, leaf mold, and sand. Handle plants carefully when inserting them in the container, because some have succulent stems and break easily. The following miniature begonias are ideal for your garden:

Begonia boweri. Green leaves with black-stitched edges. A dramatic plant.

B. 'China Boy.' Bright-green leaves, red stems, and pink blooms.

The mushroom glass terrarium offers still another dimension for small plant growing. (Photo by Matthew Barr)

B. dregei. Bronze-red maple leaves, branching habit. Picturesque growth.

B. hydrocotylifolia. Round dark-green leaves. Small and handsome.

B. 'Rosa Kugel.' Small green leaves; a wax begonia. Tiny but popular.

B. rotundifolia. Apple-green leaves, pink blooms; handsome small plant.

Ferns

Few plants can match the beauty and grace of ferns. The miniature and smaller species are especially enchanting and make perfect garden subjects. If you're fond of ferns but have had trouble growing them at windows, do try them in the terrarium garden.

Use a few ferns with other plants in a terrarium, or grow a fernery. The preparation of the fernery is the same as for other gardens. Ferns look delightful when tucked between small stones, so make careful arrangements, paying attention to shaping the soil in graceful lines. Here are the smaller ferns ideal for your terrarium:

Adiantum cuneatum (Delta maidenhair fern). Full and bushy, with somewhat large green fronds.

A. hispidulum. Bright green and graceful; stays small with pruning.

A. trichomanes (maidenhair spleenwort). Good small fern (to 8 inches) with toothed fronds.

Humata tyermannii (bear's foot fern). Often available at local florists. Small, lacy, and lovely.

Lygodium scandens (climbing fern). A climbing fern with apple-green foliage. Wiry; tiny green leaves. Excellent.

Microlepia strigosa. A small and handsome lacy fern. Good one.

All kinds of philodendrons grow under artificial light; here flood lamps are concealed in ceiling. (Photo courtesy General Electric)

Under fluorescent lamps, African violets thrive. Other gesneriads do equally well under lights. (Photo by Matthew Barr)

Incandescent track lights are fine for plants; keep lamp about 30 inches from top of plants. (Photo courtesy Halo Lighting)

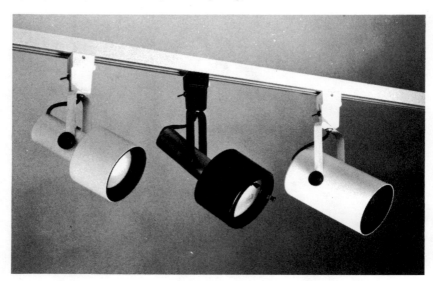

Orchids

Miniature orchids were scarce at one time; but now many are available from mail order orchid suppliers. These handsome plants have incredible flowers, some no larger than a pinhead, and others up to 2 inches in diameter. Colors range from orange to green, brown to tan. Most species are only a few inches tall.

Orchids, like gesneriads, do very well in terrariums with bright light (no sun is needed). Pot orchids in fir bark in the soil bed. Make planting pockets and fill with the bark.

Ask for orchids by botanical name (as listed here) to get the right ones. Orchids are just like jewels under glass. Try the following miniatures:

Angraecum compactum. A miracle of nature, with leaves only 2 inches long and beautiful 2-inch white flowers.

Asocentrum miniatum. Dozens of bright orange flowers on a 2-inch plant.

Broughtonia sanguinea. Solitary green leaves only a few inches tall. Branching scapes with 1-inch brick-red flowers.

B. morphologorum. A thrusting stem carries several hundred tiny yellow-brown flowers. Very unusual.

Cirrhopetalum cumingii. Tiny, to about 1 inch, with brilliant red and pink flowers in the shape of a half circle.

Gastrochilus bellinus. Leathery green foliage; yellow-white and purple-white flowers. Tiny.

Ground Creepers

Ground creepers and mosses are indispensable in the terrarium garden because they clothe the soil with graceful greenery. My favorites are Irish moss, Scotch moss, and chamomile. Besides adding beauty, mosses are useful in the terrarium because they immediately soak up excess water, thus preventing a stagnant soil.

To plant ground covers, push tiny pieces of them into soil with a dowel stick, making sure they're well inserted; if they just rest on top, they'll soon die. Here are some ground creepers and mosses to try:

Alyssum wulfenianum. Low and compact, with grayish foliage.

Anthemis nobilis (chamomile). Lovely narrow leaves. Grows easily and smells good, too.

Arenaria verna caespitosa. (Irish moss). Yellow-green vibrant color; my favorite.

Helxine soleirolii (baby's tears). Popular, with tiny dark-green leaves. Use carefully because it spreads quickly.

Mentha reguienii (Corsican mint). Small leaves and fine green accent.

Nepeta hederacea (ground ivy). Round or kidney-shaped leaves; don't confuse with English ivy.

Sagina subulata (Scotch moss). Lovely dense mat. *S. subulata* 'Aurea' is golden green.

ARTIFICIAL LIGHT GARDENS

In the fall and winter when the days are short, plants have problems growing because of a lack of enough light. Now's the time to use artificial light — fluorescent, incandescent, or a combination of both — to help plants grow through the dull months.

If you're growing only a plant or two, use one of the new grow-type lamps (shaped like reading lamps) in any fixture. Direct the light source at the plant, with the light about 30 inches from the plant. Keep the light on 12 to 14 hours a day. Floodlighting plants also helps supply needed light for plants. Floodlights with special fixtures are available as track or ceiling lamps. Use a 150-watt floodlamp, and keep it on 12 to 14 hours. Again, keep the light source 30 inches from the plant so excessive heat from the lamp won't burn foliage.

Fluorescent lamps for cart and shelf setups come in many brands. Any one of these lamps will supply the necessary rays — blue and red — plants need to grow. Fluorescent lamps come in 20 or 40 watts in various lengths, from 18 to 60 inches. Because there are so many lengths and wattages, it's best to use two 40-watt lamps for each shelf space of 2 feet. You can also use the everyday fluorescent lamps: daylight, white, and so on; daylight lamps work very well for a plant setup. Two 40-watt lamps will supply good supplemental light for most plants.

Whichever fluorescent lamps you use, leave them on 12 to 14 hours a day at a distance of 3 to 5 inches from the tops of plants. You can buy an inexpensive timer to regulate the time. And do remember that grow lights aren't miracle workers; you still must supply water, humidity, and the other usual elements of plant care.

Under ample light, plants in 5 to 6-inch pots will need water about three times a week all year, *including winter*. Ideally humidity should be between 30 and 40 percent to create the necessary balance of light, water, and temperature to make plants grow well. Usually many plants growing together will create their own humidity, but put a hygrometer in the growing area to measure the amount of moisture in the air. If there isn't enough, daily mist plants with water. If there's too much, be sure to provide adequate air circulation; sometimes all that's necessary to keep air circulating is a small electric fan going at low speed. A stuffy, stagnant air condition will quickly harm plants and cause fungous disease.

Keep temperatures between 65 and 80°F by day, with a drop of 10° at night. The cooler temperatures in the evening are essential to encourage good plant growth.

In addition to watering more frequently, follow a year-round feeding schedule for plants under lights. In fall and winter, use plant food twice a month, and three times a month the rest of the year. Use a 10-10-5 fertilizer which is neither too strong nor too weak.

In the seasonal plant lists there are many plants that will grow well under lights, but the most popular ones are gesneriads, bromeliads,

A planter of bulbs—daffodils, hyacinths, and tulips—adds beautiful color at this winter window. (Photo by Roche)

and begonias. Gesneriads include the popular African violets and columneas, kohlerias, streptocarpus, episcias, and others. Under lights these plants bear beautiful flowers.

Bromeliads are also fine plants for light gardens and include aechmeas with vase-shaped habit, neoregelias with multicolored leaves, guzmanias with rosette shape, and the popular vrieseas. Begonias are also suitable.

Geraniums, especially the miniature and dwarf types, are fine for the hobby light garden. So are orchids, cacti, and succulents. There is almost no end to the varieties of plants that can be grown under artificial light. Usually it is not a question of which plant to grow but rather its size. Generally you cannot grow tall plants because there simply isn't enough vertical space under fluorescent lamps.

BULBS FOR COLOR

Bulbs like tulips and hyacinths are easy to grow and provide color indoors from late November until April; they make any gray morning a promise of the spring that is to come. Planting the bulbs in fall is like burying treasure for the months ahead — when they burst into bloom some cold morning, you'll know what I mean.

Hyacinths, tulips, crocuses, scillas, and daffodils (narcissus) are familiar forcing bulbs. "Forcing" means handling bulbs so they'll bloom indoors ahead of their natural outdoor season. Generally, these bulbs are good for one season and then you must discard them. Bulbous

119

Hyacinths are favorite fall-flowering bulbs; here they are grown in water, but they can also be grown in soil or pebbles. (Photo by Roche)

plants such as vallota, eucharis, and many others grow all year; these plants deserve more attention from indoor gardeners and many are included (with specific growing instructions) in the plant descriptions.

You can plant bulbs in standard house plant soil or you can make your own mixture by combining half a pail of coarse sand with one pail of rich soil, adding a tablespoon each of bonemeal and lime.

Prepare the pot carefully. Use small pieces of pot shards, add a little charcoal to keep soil sweet, and be absolutely sure drainage is almost perfect. Bulbs require good drainage more than most other plants, and once growing they need lots of water. But that water should not collect and become stagnant at the bottom of the pot. The standard terra cotta pot is a good housing for bulbs.

Plant bulbs so the neck of the bulb (the tapered part) is just below soil line or the tip slightly above soil line. The size of the container depends on the size of the bulb. A large bulb (3 inches in diameter) like an amaryllis needs a 6 or 7-inch pot. You can plant six smaller bulbs like achimenes in an 8-inch pot.

Bulbs are forced in three stages. First, they need a period of rooting in a cold but not freezing cellar, closet, or garage at about 45 to 55°F (or outdoors in a trench or window-well). Second, the bulbs need a brief exposure to moderate warmth, say 60 to 65°F, with some light but no sun. The third and final stage involves moving the bulbs to a place where the temperature is 70 or 75°F and where there is bright light so they can perfect their flowers.

For indoor rooting, I put the pots in an unheated pantry where it is 45 to 50°F during the late fall months. I set planted bulbs on shelves in an airy place without light and keep them just moist. The soil shouldn't be either soggy or dry during this important rooting time.

You can also root bulbs outdoors (if you have the space). Put them in a trench deep and wide enough to accommodate the largest pot. The bottom of the pot should be about a foot below the soil surface. Cover the pots of bulbs in the trench with 2 to 3 inches of sand to keep the new leaves clean. Then fill between and over the pots with soil to ground level; spread a thick layer of oak leaves or evergreen boughs over the pots to prevent freezing.

As soon as pots are filled with roots — in six to nine weeks, depending on the type of bulb — bring them to light for the second stage of forcing, in moderate warmth not over 65°F. Pots are ready to move if roots are making their way through the drainage hole in the bottom of the pot. But first give the bulbs from the outdoors a day or two at 50°F. Water the bulbs as you do other house plants. Don't fertilize; the embryo flower has already been formed.

Before you put pots in bright light be sure tulips are up about 4 inches, the stalks of Dutch hyacinth are showing pale color, and the buds of daffodils are well up and vigorous looking.

A lovely pot of scillas decorates this table for fall; these plants grow easily and make handsome accents. (Photo by Roche)

A delightful arrangement of scillas and muscaris, this dish garden will brighten any window. (Photo by Roche)

If you don't have a garden, discard bulbs after they have bloomed; it is not possible to force them again. If you do have a garden, plant them as you normally would. After one or two years in the garden, they will recover and bloom outdoors as well as new bulbs.

Bulbs that don't need forcing include plants such as eucharis, vallotas, and smithianthas that grow all year and never need a definite rest. Other bulbous plants that don't need forcing but *do* need a definite rest after blooming are: achimenes, ornithagalum, gloxinia, cyclamen, caladium (grown for foliage), gloriosa, and rechsteineria. To rest plants, either unpot the bulbs and store them in a brown bag in cool (50°F) temperatures, or merely store the bulbs in their pots in a cool dark place. Pot bulbs in fresh soil the following year. Bulbous plants and how to grow them are in the seasonal plant descriptions.

When you buy house plants, you can see what you're buying but bulbs are an unknown quantity. How do you tell a good bulb from a bad one? You really can't. It's like buying onions or potatoes — you never really know what's inside. You must buy bulbs from reputable nurseries or from suppliers who specialize in bulbs. If you buy packaged bulbs at random places, you'll probably get good bulbs — but note the word "probably." And bulbs that come in their own little cartons, to start immediately (generally sold at supermarkets), are a dubious buy. I've tried the supermarket bulbs; I got flowers, but the quality left a great deal to be desired.

8 DECORATING THE INDOORS

IN THE FALL I start thinking about how my indoor greenery can add beauty and decorative effect during the gray months ahead. I know that during the cool and cold months I'll be in my home more and will want my surroundings to be as pleasant as possible.

ORNAMENTAL CONTAINERS

In Chapter 1 we discussed standard terra cotta pots; now we'll talk about ornamental pots for plants. I think the elegant cachepots you see in boutiques are the most decorative pots for small plants. They come in beautiful colors and designs and make even the most common plant a showpiece; use them on tables, desks, shelves, or wherever else you want pretty accents. Glazed pots are also handsome for larger plants. Just be sure they have drainage holes — some don't.

Urns and jardinières can sometimes be overbearing in a room setting, so choose them carefully. Handsome pedestal urns are usually too large for indoors; wood and stone pots usually look out of place in the average home. Glazed Oriental pots are expensive but stunning in special places that need rich color. The attractive blue-glazed tubs are really for very large plants, where you want to make a bold statement.

Round Chinese ceramic pots in various sizes and blue or green colors are ideal for spot accent on a table or desk. These pots can be extremely elaborate or very simple. Be careful of brass pots and metal tubs. Toxic salts can build up in brass containers, and I have had some bad experiences with metal tubs; eventually the paint peeled from the outside of the containers.

Don't overlook bonsai pots, which have a certain simplicity and elegance. The colors are usually browns or blacks, and most bonsai pots come with their own individual saucers. Hanging plant containers are high on the list of decorative items used by designers, and plants at eye level do look handsome. Unfortunately, containers for these plants are not always practical; most are really cover-ups rather than pots to plant in.

If you have a container you're dubious about, such as a brass pot or an elaborate urn that doesn't have drainage holes, slip potted plants into them and cover the tops with moss rather than potting directly into the containers.

PLACES FOR PLANTS

Where you put a plant does make a difference in a room's décor. Move small plants around to decorate tables and desks. Use large plants as substitutes for furniture, to guide traffic, as screens, and so on. If you're using plants on tables, be sure there's adequate protection against moisture seepage. One special small plant in a cachepot always looks good as a table accessory, but a group of three pots of the same size (if the table is large) can be really striking. Don't use any container that has a brash color which might upset the room scheme, of course. White is always acceptable; other colors depend on the room itself.

One tall plant like a palm is a handsome vertical accent near windows, and against a wall it can take the place of a picture. A row of plants at one end of a window wall is dramatically effective. Use distinctive pottery here because the plant and container become part of the design of the room. A large plant with graceful habit, like a schefflera, goes well next to an end table. But don't put a single plant in a corner, because one plant in a corner looks just like a plant in a corner — there's no relation to the rest of the room. However, a large

Baskets are often used for pot plants; the usual procedure is merely to slip the potted plant into the cover-up container. (Photo by Matthew Barr)

124

This recreation room is decorated with pot plants. Note the handsome marriage of indoors and outdoors. (Photo by Clark)

plant with a few small ones around it creates an island of greenery in the corner.

If you can, put plants at different levels in a room. This means positioning plants on pedestals or small stools. Two or three plants on two or three tables of varying heights creates a handsome picture. People frequently put plants on the floor next to a sofa, but this is a bad place for them because they don't relate to the room. Use a table and a lamp next to your couch; bookcases or étagères are the places where small trailing plants will soften the harsh lines of contemporary furniture and add softness to a room.

Many people naturally put plants on windowsills because of the fine light. But a jumble of plants on a windowsill is not really handsome. If you're going to have a window garden, select appropriate shelves, use distinctive pots of one color, and create a garden, not a jungle.

Do plants belong in kitchens and bathrooms? Indeed they do — they look good and add a pleasant color in these often barren areas. We spend a good deal of time in kitchens, so kitchens are ideal spots for miniature and small plants. Use groups of plants in pots rather than a single pot that will seem incongruous to the whole. There's rarely room in kitchens for large plants, but there are many small plants that work well. And plants thrive on the humidity from cooking and running water; they seem to grow better in kitchens than in other rooms. The bathroom is also a perfect source of humidity, and plants in the bathroom relieve the severe lines and antiseptic look. If you have space, use large, graceful plants like palms; otherwise concentrate on a few flowering plants.

ACCENT AREAS

Accent areas can be kitchen windows, bathroom corners, living rooms — anywhere that you want color and emphasis. You can create a veritable tropical garden if you group plants and have them at varying heights on tables. No matter where your accent area, you must work carefully with plants. Use small-leaved and large-leaved plants to achieve the varied effect of outdoor landscaping indoors. Look at the outdoor summer garden display or walk through a park. You don't see only green; you see shades of green in a handsome monochromatic scheme.

Pay attention to heights in accent areas. Plants all the same height create a barrier; small, medium, and tall plants together add depth and dimension to the color and texture.

HANGING GARDENS

Hanging gardens are a delightful addition at windows for autumn and the coming winter days — something green and handsome to greet the eye of the visitor and to keep up your spirits. Gardens at eye level are always on display, never lost in corners or on shelves and windowsills.

Watering hanging plants is somewhat more difficult than watering plants at standard levels. How do you get to the plant to water it? And there's always the possibility of water dripping on floors. The right container can help the latter problem, and most people like hanging plants enough to put up with some inconvenience.

The container for hanging plants must have some device on or attached to it to hold excess water that drains from soil. Some molded plastic pots now include an attached saucer. but the terra cotta pot doesn't have this feature. With terra cotta pots you'll have to use clip-on hangers, which attach to the rim of the saucer and thus hold the saucer and the pot. The arrangement isn't ideal — occasionally a plant can fall so be sure hangers are securely fastened.

Other, more sophisticated containers are the rattan or wooden cover-ups. Some of these are just cover-ups, but others have an iron insert that holds the rim of the pot, as well as a circular iron base on which a saucer can be placed. Avoid the simple cover-up that's nothing more than a basket; it's almost impossible to fit drip saucers inside them. You can also take almost any pot and suspend it in fishnet or macramé, but again, you'll have the problem of excess water dripping on the floors.

The old-fashioned inexpensive wire baskets for hanging plants are excellent as long as they're suspended over tile or concrete floors (water won't affect tile or concrete). Of course, you can use any container and take it down every time you want to water the plant, but this is more a chore than a pleasure.

Dizygotheca is a favorite indoor tree; it is very graceful and can be used almost anywhere in the home for vertical accent. (Photo courtesy Martin Des)

Once you have the container, you need some device to suspend it from the ceiling. Chains are generally the answer. Or use rope or monofilament wire. No matter what you use, be sure it can support the weight of the plant and pot. An 8-inch pot filled with soil can weigh over 50 pounds, and falling pots are certainly a hazard to both people and the plant.

Attachments for ceilings are easy to find, including some elaborate ones, but actually all you need is a simple eyebolt or screw-eye hook. When you install the hook, try to hit a stud in the ceiling so the screw has something to grasp. If this isn't possible, insert the screw part of the hook into a toggle bolt (ask your hardware dealer about them.)

Hanging plants exposed to air, good circulation, and light will dry out faster than plants at windowsills and other areas. Even in winter when many plants are grown somewhat dry, plants in the air need a

A built-in planter is accented with nicodemia, a fine indoor tree. At the base of the plant are marantas, pileas, and other smaller plants. (Photo by Ken Molino)

soil that is damp to the touch. You can also feed plants more than you ordinarily would, although in winter do reduce feeding to about once a month. Use a 10-10-5 plant food for both foliage and flowering plants.

An important part of a successful hanging garden display is keeping plants trimmed and groomed. Don't be afraid to cut away errant leaves and stems; train plants to specific shapes so they look well from all angles. Cutting and trimming also encourages new growth. But do the trimming in spring or summer, not in fall or winter.

Although you can grow almost any plant in a hanging container, cascading or bushy plants are the most appropriate; upright growers sometimes look awkward.

Many plants in the seasonal lists make good hanging subjects. Here, though, are some of the best:

Ferns

If you hang ferns they will grow better and look more handsome than if grown at windows or on shelves. Ferns have a natural rosette growth, and when mature fronds become pendent and graceful, a hanging container suits them very well. The best plants in this group are the Boston ferns with their bright green fronds.

Chlorophytum

The spider plant is an old favorite because if necessary it can survive drought. (It has its own water storage roots.) The beauty of the plants in the chlorophytum family is that they are grassy and graceful and "throw out" small plantlets on long stems. A well-grown plant may have two dozen pendent stems with tiny plants, and this trailing effect is at its best in baskets.

Tradescantias and Zebrinas

Here are two plant groups with natural trailers, some growing six feet long. It is a waste to grow these plants unless they are in hanging containers where one can see their true beauty. The plants grow rapidly and come in an array of colors. Some varieties have wine-red foliage, others green-and-white striped leaves.

A column of ferns in wire baskets is an elegant addition in this kitchen window garden. (Photo by Matthew Barr)

Cissus

These plants (kangaroo ivy and grape ivy) have scalloped leaves and trailing habit. They grow quickly and provide a green screen of beauty in baskets. Because they can do equally well in sun or shade they have become a familiar indoor plant. Like the plant called wandering Jew, the cissus plants are absolutely at their best in the air and can grow to great proportions.

Asparagus sprengeri

Also known as the emerald fern, this single plant is a bounty of color for basket growing. They like large pots and plenty of water and when hung they grow large and fronds assume a beautiful hanging pattern. The feathery loveliness of *A. sprengeri* is hard to surpass; if I had but one plant to recommend for basket growing, this would be my choice.

Ferns also do well as hanging plants; this davallia is growing nicely. Plants at eye level can be seen from all angles. (Photo by Matthew Barr)

9 WHAT TO DO IN FALL

BEGONIAS

Begonias will still be growing during this time. Most have a long season of growth; some even put out new leaves in winter.

Water and Light: Water as you did in spring and summer; wet soil and then allow it to dry out between waterings. Give the plants all possible light; some sun is especially beneficial now, even for rex types.

Temperature and Humidity: Maintain a humidity of 20 to 30 percent; most begonias enjoy moisture in the air. Average home temperatures are fine, with a slight drop at night.

Feeding: Reduce feeding; apply food only once every six weeks or, if you are cautious, stop feeding altogether.

BROMELIADS

With gray days it is imperative to give more attention to bromeliads, because some will be starting new growth and others getting ready for a rest cycle. Specific instructions are in the plant descriptions.

Water and Light: Keep soil evenly moist; water twice a week, keeping the "vases" filled with water at all times. Most bromeliads are in 6 or 7-inch pots so a general watering schedule can be adopted for all. The more light you can give bromeliads now, the better they will be next year, so select bright places for them.

Temperature and Humidity: As artificial heat is turned on, be sure to supply adequate humidity for bromeliads. This is the best time to put plants on pebble trays (pebbles kept moist) and to use a small space humidifier if you have it.

Feeding: Do not feed plants at all; bromeliads react unfavorably to most plant foods. These are nature's air plants so let them grow naturally.

Note: Get your plants ready for the gray months ahead by seeing that they are well groomed — all dead leaves and flower bracts removed — and that leaves are clean. Sponge foliage with a damp cloth; this is imperative for bromeliads because they are air plants.

131

BULBS

This is the season when so many bulbs are started: daffodil, crocus, amaryllis, veltheimia, vallota, and many more. Indeed, one could spend weeks now getting bulbs ready for the indoor garden to have a colorful succession of bloom for the months ahead.

Water and Light: Bulbs that are just started need a barely-damp-to-the-touch soil, neither moist nor dry. These plants also require coolness; most are forced for indoor bloom.

Temperature and Humidity: See individual bulbous plants in the fall plant list and refer to Chapter 7.

Feeding: Do not feed during this season.

CACTI

In the autumn months cacti may still bear some flowers, but usually the plants are going into a rest period and need special care.

Water and Light: Reduce watering and keep soil just barely moist to the touch. You can keep plants in sun or move them to a bright window as they prepare for winter.

Temperature and Humidity: Provide good ventilation; average home temperatures and humidity will suit most cacti. In other words, don't fuss with the plants but allow them to grow naturally.

Feeding: If you have been feeding cacti, stop now because excessive feeding can result in forced growth that will be gnarled and useless.

FERNS

Ferns are at their best now after summer growth. While a few new fronds may be starting, for the most part active growth is over and plants are starting their rest period.

Water and Light: Reduce watering to twice a week; keep soil evenly moist, never soggy, and be sure plants have a good bright location. Plants can tolerate bright light now to ripen growth.

Temperature and Humidity: Keep ferns out of direct drafts and blasts of heat from heating registers or radiators. Plants need a somewhat lower temperature, about 70°F. Stop misting plants; too many cloudy days and excessive humidity can do more harm than good.

Feeding: Avoid feeding plants as autumn comes into full swing, but trim and groom them. Remove dead fronds and straggly growth.

GERANIUMS

Enjoy these lovely plants now; many are in full bloom and offer much beauty. Trim and groom plants frequently; faded flowers should be picked and discarded, never left on plants.

Water and Light: Keep soil evenly moist and be sure plants are in bright light or in sun.

Temperature and Humidity: Provide a temperature of 60 to 65°F for the plants; move them close to windows where it is cooler. Keep humidity at a 20 to 30 percent level but don't spray plants.

Feeding: Reduce feeding now; make applications occasionally, say every month or less, for plants in 5 or 6-inch pots.

GESNERIADS

Many gesneriads will have stopped blooming now, but the popular African violets start their season.

Water and Light: Keep soil evenly moist and give plants bright light; this is especially important in the fall. While gesneriads do not like direct sun, they do need bright light to prosper.

Temperature and Humidity: Temperature should be somewhat lower — about 68°F — for best results, although plants won't die if it is somewhat higher. Ventilation should be good, so be sure there is fresh air or provide a small fan.

Feeding: Reduce feeding to once every six weeks; use a 10-10-5 fertilizer.

Note: Gesneriads grow well under artificial light.

FLOWERING PLANTS

There are flowering plants for all seasons, as you will discover in the plant descriptions. Some are finished blooming now but others are just starting to bear color.

Water and Light: Keep soil evenly moist, neither wet nor dry, but not as moist as in summer. Be sure plants are in good sunlight so they can prosper.

Temperature and Humidity: Most flowering plants like warmth, so try to maintain a temperature range of 75 to 80°F. Keep humidity at 30 percent. Try to provide a good circulation of air for the plants. Flowering plants are more finicky about air circulation than foliage types.

Feeding: It is time to reduce feeding. If you were feeding plants twice a month, reduce it to once a month. If you were feeding them once a month, reduce it to one application every six weeks.

FOLIAGE PLANTS

In the fall adopt a new set of watering and feeding rules for foliage plants. While it is true that these plants grow all year, there is still a quiet period; some new cultural rules are in order.

Water and Light: Water plants thoroughly and then allow them to dry out between waterings. Place plants in good light; some sun is beneficial for them.

Temperature and Humidity: Your foliage plants will do well in average home temperatures during the day, a few degrees less at night. Do, however, increase humidity as artificial heating is started. Mist plants frequently.

Feeding: Feed foliage plants, but sparsely, perhaps once every sixth or seventh watering. You do not want to force plants into growth but rather maintain a balanced nutrient content in the soil.

ORCHIDS

In fall many orchids will be blooming. The plants are well worth their space in the indoor garden now. Flowers of most orchids last four to six weeks and the blooms are lovely. They can also be used for cutting; put them in vases of water for unusual home decoration.

Water and Light: The orchids that bloom in this season (they are in the plant descriptions) will need a slight drying out as September comes; give them a three to four week rest, keeping the growing medium just barely moist. As soon as you see the flower spikes emerging, start watering every other day but never allow the medium to become soggy or the spikes will rot. It is quite safe at this time of year to put orchids in sun; it is not as intense as in summer and most types benefit greatly from good light.

Temperature and Humidity: As opposed to spring and summer when it was vital to provide good humidity for plants, now they can fare quite well with less, say 20 to 30 percent. Too much humidity coupled with dark days can create fungous disease, so stop misting plants entirely. But keep air circulation good; a fresh flow of air is vital.

Feeding: Do not feed orchids now; they do not need it. Keep plants well groomed. Pick any faded flowers and trim leaves if necessary; some may have developed scorch marks from intense summer sun.

PALMS

If you thought you enjoyed your palms in summer, you will like them even more now because they are mature, green, and lush.

Water and Light: Reduce watering now; if you watered three times a week before, reduce moisture to once or twice a week, and keep soil just evenly moist. In fall, soggy soil can kill palms. Bright light is still needed.

Temperature and Humidity: You can stop misting the plants now but keep wiping leaves with a damp cloth to keep them clean and good-looking. Average home temperatures and humidity are fine.

Feeding: If you have been feeding your plants, stop feeding now. Palms go into a rest period in the fall and forcing growth can harm them.

SUCCULENTS

You will appreciate the beauty of the succulents now if you have some echeverias or aloes indoors. They are sculptural plants that are distinctive from other house plants.

Water and Light: In spring and summer I suggested keeping soil evenly moist; now it is time to reduce watering so the soil is just barely moist. Don't let soil dry out completely, but rather keep it damp to the touch. You can put plants in sun now — it is not strong enough to scorch leaves — or leave them in bright light.

Temperature and Humidity: There are no special requirements about temperature or humidity during this season. Plants can tolerate a wide range of temperatures and do not seem to be harmed by low humidity. Indeed, high humidity coupled with gray days can cause fungous disease. Again, provide good circulation of air.

Feeding: Even if you are tempted, do not feed plants at this time of year.

HOUSE PLANTS FOR FALL

AECHMEA CALYCULATA
This 20-inch bromeliad with green striped leaves bears a crown of vivid yellow flowers in spring or in early fall. It needs a bright place at the window. Keep the potting medium moderately moist and be sure the "vase" of the plant is filled with water. Pot in fine-grade fir bark.
All Year: Follow fall schedule.

AECHMEA FASCIATA   silver urn plant
Perhaps the most popular of all bromeliads, the silver urn plant grows to 30 inches and bears a splendid crown of small blue and pink flower heads. It does best in bright light and a moderately moist potting medium, but can survive in moderate or even low light. Pot in medium-grade fir bark.
All Year: Follow fall schedule.

AGLAONEMA MODESTUM   Chinese evergreen
This lovely foliage plant grows to about 28 inches with waxy dark-green foliage. Keep it evenly moist in either moderate or low light.
Winter: Dry out slightly. Bright light.
Spring: Keep evenly moist. Bright light.
Summer: Provide ample water. Bright light.

AGLAONEMA ROBELINII
Perhaps the most popular of the aglaonemas, this 36-inch plant has blue-green leaves and can survive almost any situation, but for best results keep it in a moderate or bright place and let the soil dry out between waterings.
Winter: Dry out between waterings. Bright light.
Spring: Keep evenly moist. Moderate light.
Summer: Keep evenly moist. Moderate light.

ALLAMANDA CATHARTICA
This large evergreen climber, to 60 inches, is known for its 7-inch golden yellow flowers, which usually appear in early fall. Its disadvantage is that it takes a lot of space and needs a large container. Give full sun and plenty of water during growth. A good one for the adventurer.
Winter: Keep barely moist. Sun.
Spring: Cut back to 6 inches; repot. Provide ample water. Sun.
Summer: Provide ample water. Sun.

ALLOPHYTUM MEXICANUM   Mexican foxglove
Here is a charming 10-inch plant with long leathery dark-green leaves and fragrant tubular lavender flowers that start blooming in summer and continue into fall. The plant needs all the sun you can give it; keep soil evenly moist. Good under lights.
Winter: Dry out somewhat. Sun.
Spring: Keep soil evenly moist. Sun.
Summer: Provide ample water. Sun.

ASPARAGUS PLUMOSUS
This is an upright grower, to about 24 inches. Its feathery fronds make lovely color at the autumn window. Keep soil evenly moist and give the plant bright light.
Winter: Follow fall schedule.
Spring: Follow fall schedule.
Summer: Increase moisture. Bright light.

Aechmea calyculata

Aechmea fasciata

Aglaonema modestum

Aglaonema robelinii

Allamanda cathartica

Allophytum mexicanum

Asparagus plumosus

ASTROPHYTUM ASTERIAS
star cactus

A 3-inch globe, this spineless cactus is easy to grow. Occasionally it may bear reddish-yellow flowers if it is in sun. Keep the soil just barely moist.

Winter: Keep barely moist. Sun.
Spring: Increase waterings. Sun.
Summer: Provide ample water. Sun.

BEGONIA ALLEYRI

This is one of the hairy-leaved begonias that grows to 30 inches, with dark-green leaves with white hairs and clusters of lovely pale pink flowers. The plant performs superbly in sun. Keep the soil evenly moist; overwatering can cause rot. Ideal for basket growing.

Winter: Follow fall schedule.
Spring: Increase water somewhat. Sun.
Summer: Provide ample water. Sun.

BEGONIA 'ELSIE M FREY'

This 36-inch begonia has splendid metallic green red-lined leaves and beautiful pink flowers. The plant needs good sunlight and even moisture; easy to grow. Splendid as a hanging plant.

Winter: Keep evenly moist. Sun.
Spring: Keep evenly moist. Bright light.
Summer: Provide ample water. Bright light.

BEGONIA ERYTHROPHYLLA
beefsteak begonia

A popular small begonia growing to 24 inches, this plant has round leaves, green on top, red underneath. The beefsteak begonia likes a bright place; allow the soil to dry out between waterings. Good dish garden plant.

Winter: Follow fall schedule.
Spring: Increase waterings. Sun.
Summer: Keep evenly moist. Bright light.

BLECHNUM OCCIDENTALE

This lovely fern, growing to about 30 inches, is seldom seen; it has somewhat stiff fronds and a tree habit. Blechnum needs a bright location; keep the soil evenly moist and never soggy. An easy plant that should be grown more.

Winter: Follow fall schedule.
Spring: Increase waterings somewhat. Bright light.
Summer: Keep evenly moist. Moderate light.

BRASSAVOLA GLAUCA

A 10-inch orchid with succulent leathery leaves and large waxy-white fragrant flowers. Grow the plant in large-grade fir bark kept almost dry. If you want flowers, be sure that *B. glauca* has sun.

Winter: Grow somewhat dry. Sun.
Spring: Increase moisture. Sun.
Summer: Allow to dry out somewhat to encourage buds. Sun.

BRASSAVOLA NODOSA
lady-of-the-night

With succulent grassy foliage, to 10 inches, this fine orchid bears many highly scented white flowers. It needs good sun; keep the fir bark just barely moist.

Winter: Grow somewhat dry. Sun.
Spring: Increase moisture. Sun.
Summer: Allow to dry out somewhat. Sun.

Astrophytum asterias

Begonia alleyri

Begonia 'Elsie M. Frey'

Begonia erythrophylla

Blechnum occidentale

Brassavola glauca

Brassavola nodosa

CALATHEA CONCINNA

Here is an exquisite foliage plant from Brazil that grows to 16 inches and has dark-green feather designs running into deeper green with purple underneath. It requires good light but no sun. Be sure the soil is evenly moist. Rather a difficult plant to grow, but the multicolored almost iridescent leaves make it well worth the effort.

All Year: Follow fall schedule.

CALATHEA MAKOYANA

This fine 40-inch foliage plant has olive-green and pink leaves, beautifully veined with silver. It requires good light but no sun and should be kept evenly moist. Somewhat temperamental, so move it around a bit if it does not do well in one place.

All Year: Follow fall schedule.

CALATHEA ROSEO PICTA

Perhaps the most popular of the calatheas because it is readily available, this 12-inch dark-green-and-red-leaved plant offers much color for autumn. Like other members of the family, it needs bright light but no sun and an evenly moist soil.

All Year: Follow fall schedule.

CAMPANULA FRAGILIS

This basket plant, a somewhat trailing one growing to 20 inches, has pale-blue flowers. It requires good ventilation and bright light, but generally little, if any, sun. Allow soil to dry out between waterings.

Winter: Follow fall schedule.
Spring: Keep evenly moist. Bright light.
Summer: Keep evenly moist. Bright light.

CAMPANULA ISOPHYLLUS   star of Bethlehem

Perhaps the most popular of the campanulas is this white-flowering 20-inch beauty, which is covered with flowers from August until November. Quite a cheerful sight for autumn. The plant needs good ventilation and bright light. Let soil dry out between waterings. Pick off flowers as they fade; seed formation reduces bloom. Good basket plant.

Winter: Cut back to 5 inches; repot. Water sparsely. Bright light.
Spring: Increase moisture. Bright light. Keep cool.
Summer: Keep evenly moist. Bright light. Grow cool.

CAPSICUM ANNUUM   red pepper plant

This delightful fall plant with little red peppers is always a welcome sight on gray days. It grows to about 20 inches and needs full sun and an evenly moist soil. Try to grow as cool as possible (60° F); fruit drops in a hot room. Although lasting only the season, the red pepper plant is still worthwhile. Many varieties available.

CARYOTA MITIS   fishtail palm

This lovely 40-inch palm has become very popular, and rightfully so. It has graceful, glossy green scalloped fronds that resemble fishtails. The plant is really easy to grow in bright or moderate light: keep soil evenly moist. Possibly one of the best indoor palms.

All Year: Follow fall schedule.

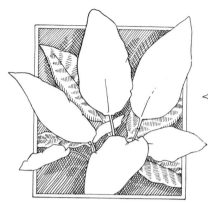

Calathea concinna

Calathea makoyana

Calathea roseo picta

Campanula fragilis

Campanula isophyllus

Capsicum annuum

Caryota mitis

CARYOTA PLUMOSA

Not as well known as the fishtail palm, this caryota, growing to 48 inches, has bright-green leathery fronds on a single trunk. It requires only bright light and an evenly moist soil to be at its best.

All Year: Follow fall schedule.

CEPHALOCEREUS PALMERI   old man cactus

A 12 to 20-inch desert plant, the old man cactus is more bizarre than beautiful, with white hairs and somewhat barrel-shaped. It requires a sunny location and a rather dry soil. It seems to grow untended, and, though very slow-growing, it will be with you for many years.

Winter: Keep barely moist. Sun.
Spring: Increase moisture. Sun.
Summer: Keep evenly moist. Sun.

CHAMAEDOREA ELEGANS   parlor palm

Here is a shade-loving palm from Central America that can grow to 60 inches. It is graceful, colorful, and easy to grow. Keep it in moderate or low light with an evenly moist soil.

Winter: Dry out between waterings. Bright light.
Spring: Increase moisture. Bright light.
Summer: Provide ample moisture. Moderate light.

CHAMAEDOREA ERUMPENS   bamboo palm

Another fine plant, the bamboo palm can grow to 60 inches. It has the character of bamboo with broad green fronds. Give it bright light but no sunshine and keep the soil quite wet.

Winter: Dry out between waterings. Bright light.
Spring: Increase moisture. Bright light.
Summer: Provide ample water. Bright light.

CHRYSANTHEMUM

These are the familiar garden flowers that can be grown indoors as well as outdoors. Plants grow to about 20 inches and come in an array of colors. To make chrysanthemums last as long as possible indoors, put them in a cool place (60° F)) with some morning or afternoon sun and keep the soil evenly moist. After flowers fade, cut back stems to 2 inches and set plants in a frost-free garage, with soil kept barely moist until spring. Then, if you have a garden, you can set the plants out to grow again.

CORDYLINE TERMINALIS   ti-plant

A 36-inch palmlike plant, the ti-plant is graceful and attractive for fall. It is relatively easy to grow and only needs a bright airy location. Keep soil moderately moist. The miracle Hawaiian log that comes to life in a dish of water is a member of this family.

Winter: Keep soil evenly moist. Bright light.
Spring: Keep soil evenly moist. Bright light.
Summer: Provide ample water. Bright light.

CRASSULA ARBORESCENS

These succulent plants grow to about 14 inches and make ideal house plants because they tolerate lack of moisture. Generally gray or blue in color, *C. arborescens* has branching stems and little rosettes of leaves. Give it bright light or full sun and let soil dry out between waterings.

Winter: Dry out between waterings. Sun.
Spring: Dry out between waterings. Sun.
Summer: Increase moisture. Bright light.

Caryota plumosa

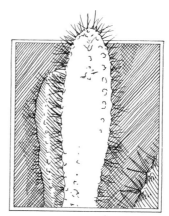

Cephalocereus palmeri

Chamaedorea elegans

Chamaedorea erumpens

Chrysanthemum

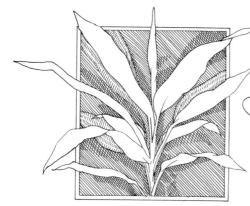

Cordyline terminalis

Crassula arborescens

CRASSULA ARGENTEA   jade tree
The jade tree grows to 48 inches and has branching stems of glossy green
leaves. It needs bright or moderate light but no sun, and a soil that is
moderately moist. Easy to grow.

Winter: Dry out between waterings. Bright light.
Spring: Keep evenly moist. Bright light.
Summer: Keep evenly moist. Bright light.

CROCUS
The familiar crocus with its purple flowers is available as a gift plant from
florist shops. It is colorful and delightful but will only be with you for a few
weeks. Grow it as cool as possible (60° F) and keep soil evenly moist.
See Chapter 7 for more information.

CYCAS REVOLUTA   sago palm
This tough, slow-growing plant, to 60 inches, has leathery green fronds and is
quite handsome. Grow it in moderate light and keep the soil evenly moist.
Sunlight will harm the plant, so be sure it is protected from direct rays.

Winter: Dry out between waterings. Moderate light.
Spring: Keep evenly moist. Moderate light.
Summer: Keep evenly moist. Low light.

CYRTOMIUM FALCATUM   holly fern
This fine fern grows to about 60 inches, the green fronds resembling holly
leaves. it is a handsome palm that does very well indoors and can take
considerable abuse; however, optimum conditions — moderate light and
evenly moist soil — produce a better plant.

Winter: Follow fall schedule.
Spring: Increase waterings somewhat. Moderate light.
Summer: Keep evenly moist. Moderate light.

DIZYGOTHECA ELEGANTISSIMA   false aralia
The false aralia is a graceful treelike plant, to about 60 inches, with dark
green-brown palmlike leaves. It makes a fine fall accent. Young plants are
very difficult to cultivate so it is best to start with a two or three-year
specimen. Don't overwater. It is much better to allow the soil to dry out
between waterings. Place in bright light.

All Year: Follow fall schedule.

ERANTHEMUM NERVOSUM   blue sage
I think this is one of the nicest blue-flowering plants for autumn. Growing to
about 30 inches, it is an outdoor plant but will adapt to indoor growing
conditions. Give it full sun and keep soil evenly moist. Overwatering will
cause leaf drop. Small plants bloom as readily as large ones.

Winter: Keep somewhat dry. Sun.
Spring: Increase moisture. Sun.
Summer: Keep evenly moist. Bright light.

EXACUM AFFINE   German violet
With small fragrant blue flowers, growing to 24 inches, this plant starts
flowering in September and reaches its peak in January. Give German
violets full sun and keep soil evenly moist. Cut back after flowering to ensure
future bloom. Fine plant for terrariums.

Winter: Keep barely moist. Sun.
Spring: Cut back to 4 inches; repot. Provide even moisture. Sun.
Summer: Keep evenly moist. Bright light.

Crassula argentea

Crocus

Cycas revoluta

Cyrtomium falcatum

Dizygotheca elegantissima

Eranthemum nervosum

Exacum affine

FATSIA JAPONICA
This decorative plant grows to 60 inches and has dark-green ivy leaves on graceful stems. It withstands almost any condition and survives for years. Keep soil wet but never soggy. It will grow in low light or any interior spot where most plants would perish.
Winter: Dry out between waterings. Moderate light.
Spring: Increase moisture. Low light.
Summer: Keep evenly moist. Low light.

FATSIA VARIEGATA
Similar to *F. japonica*, this is a variegated form with medium-green leaves edged with white. It is prettier but more difficult to grow and is quite sensitive to overwatering. Try it if you have the time to give it extra care.
Winter: Dry out between waterings. Moderate light.
Spring: Increase moisture. Low light.
Summer: Keep evenly moist. Low light.

FITTONIA VERSCHAFFELTII
Like most fittonias, this handsome 16-inch plant is grown for its foliage — green leaves reticulated with red veins. It needs low light. Allow soil to dry out between waterings. Somewhat difficult to grow, it is certainly worth the time.
Winter: Keep barely moist. Low light.
Spring: Keep barely moist. Low light.
Summer: Keep evenly moist. Low light.

FREESIA
The lovely fragrant flowers of freesias are well known. Growing to 10 inches, freesias are started from corms; place five or six slightly below the soil line and grow very cool (55° F). When foliage starts to grow move to a bright place. Excellent cut flowers but not easy to grow.
See Chapter 7 for more information.

GEOGANTHUS UNDATUS
Geoganthus is a large plant, growing to 40 inches, with big leaves of velvety texture. It is a temperamental plant that needs high humidity (40 percent) and must be protected from drafts. Keep soil just evenly moist and give it bright light. Grow it only if you have time for it, because extra attention will be needed.
All Year: Follow fall schedule.

HAWORTHIA FASCIATA
This small foliage plant, growing to about 10 inches, is an erect rosette with 1½-inch dark-green incurved leaves banded with white. It is a handsome succulent plant that will grow in shade. Give it plenty of water in summer. Good for dish gardens.
Winter: Keep barely moist. Sun.
Spring: Keep evenly moist. Sun.
Summer: Keep evenly moist. Sun.

HAWORTHIA MARGARITIFERA
A low-growing rosette about 6 inches across, this haworthia has sharply pointed leaves with white granules and occasionally will bear sprays of flowers indoors. It requires bright light or sun and plenty of water.
Winter: Keep barely moist. Sun.
Spring: Keep evenly moist. Sun.
Summer: Give plenty of water. Bright light.

Fatsia japonica

Fatsia variegata

Fittonia verschaffeltii

Freesia

Geoganthus undatus

Haworthia fasciata

Haworthia margaritifera

HEDYCHIUM CORONARIUM
ginger lily

This sweetly scented flowering plant has large leaves and grows to about 60 inches. The fragrant flowers appear in late summer and early fall. This is an excellent plant for a sunny corner. Give it plenty of water but reduce moisture when bloom time is over.

Winter: Keep barely moist. Sun.
Spring: Increase waterings. Sun.
Summer: Provide ample water. Sun.

HIBISCUS COOPERI

This is an unusual hibiscus growing to 30 inches, with variegated leaves and small red flowers. It needs plenty of sun and water.

All Year: Follow fall schedule.

HIBISCUS ROSA-SINENSIS
rose-of-China

Well known for its outdoor beauty, the hibiscus, growing to 48 inches, can be a tub plant indoors. It bears large single or double blooms in red, yellow, pink, or white, blooming throughout the year, with perhaps the most abundant bloom in spring. Grow in large pots in full sun; give the plant plenty of water (they are greedy). Prune back hard after blooming and the plant will quickly grow again. Fine plant if you have the space for it. Many varieties available.

Winter: Keep evenly moist. Sun.
Spring: Cut back to 10 inches; repot. Provide ample water. Sun.
Summer: Provide ample water. Sun.

HOHENBERGIA RIDLEYII

A bromeliad growing to 48 inches, *H. ridleyii,* a beautiful apple-green rosette, bears tall stems with vividly colored flower bracts. The plant needs bright light and the "vase" of the plant should be filled with water at all times. Keep the potting medium — equal part of fir bark and soil — just barely moist.

All Year: Follow fall schedule.

HOHENBERGIA STELLATA

Similar to *H. Ridleyii* but somewhat easier to grow, this bromeliad has a diameter of 60 inches. It bears vividly colored flower bracts. Treat it the same as above.

All Year: Follow fall schedule.

HOWEA BALMOREANA
kentia palm

An indestructible palm, to 60 inches, the kentia is decorative with graceful fronds. It requires low or moderate light; keep the soil evenly moist. The plant does best when potbound, and mature specimens, although expensive, are worthy of a place in any room.

Winter: Dry out slightly. Moderate light.
Spring: Increase waterings. Moderate light.
Summer: Keep evenly moist, almost wet. Moderate light.

HOWEA FOSTERIANA

Another fine palm, sometimes called paradise palm, that grows to about 40 inches. It has waxy dark-green fronds and is not as graceful as the kentia palm. Grow in low or moderate light and keep the soil evenly moist.

Winter: Dry out slightly. Moderate light.
Spring: Increase waterings. Bright light.
Summer: Provide ample water. Bright light.

Hedychium coronarium

Hibiscus cooperi

Hibiscus rosa-sinensis

Hohenbergia ridleyii

Hohenbergia stellata

Howea balmoreana

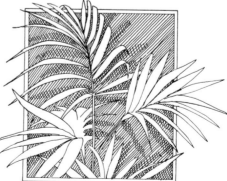

Howea fosteriana

JASMINUM HUMILE

This bushy jasmine has lovely scented yellow flowers. It is a vining plant that can grow to 60 inches. Grow in sun with evenly moist soil, and mist foliage occasionally to keep it free of insects. Not easy to grow but certainly worth a try.

Winter: Follow fall schedule.
Spring: Follow fall schedule.
Summer: Increase waterings. Sun.

JASMINUM OFFICINALE GRANDIFLORA   poet's jasmine

This shrubby, ferny vine that can grow to 60 inches has large white flowers. It needs a bright place and plenty of water. The scented flowers will perfume an entire room. Desirable but somewhat difficult to grow.

All Year: Follow fall schedule.

JASMINUM SAMBAC

Somewhat smaller than the other jasmines mentioned, this is a shrubby plant, to about 36 inches, with white flowers. It requires a sunny location and an evenly moist soil. If you want only one jasmine this would be the type to grow.

Winter: Follow fall schedule.
Spring: Increase waterings. Sun.
Summer: Keep evenly moist. Sun.

LAELIA ANCEPS

A showy orchid that grows to 30 inches with 4-inch pink flowers, *L. anceps* is a great indoor plant. Give it as much sun as possible, allowing it to dry out between waterings. Grow in medium-grade fir bark.

Winter: Keep somewhat dry. Sun.
Spring: Provide even moisture. Sun.
Summer: Allow to dry out somewhat to encourage buds. Sun.

LAELIA GOULDIANA

Another fine orchid, this one has rose-magenta flowers about 5 inches across. The plant needs good sunlight and plenty of water. Grow in medium-grade fir bark.

All Year: Follow fall schedule.

LIVISTONA CHINENSIS   Chinese fan palm

A robust palm, growing to about 40 inches, livistona has a solitary trunk and big fan-shaped leaves. It requires bright light and an evenly moist soil. Although not often seen, this is an excellent palm for room decoration.

Winter: Dry out between waterings. Sun.
Spring: Increase moisture. Bright light.
Summer: Provide ample moisture. Bright light.

MAHERNIA VERTICILLATA   honeybells

This is a 20-inch rangy plant but worthwhile because it bears yellow flowers now. The plant needs sun to bear flowers; soak soil and let dry out before watering again. While not spectacular, mahernia has charm and makes a fine plant for basket containers.

All Year: Follow fall schedule.

Jasminum humile

Jasminum officinale grandiflora

Jasminum sambac

Laelia anceps

Laelia gouldiana

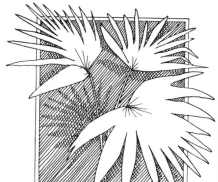

Livistona chinensis

Mahernia verticillata

MARANTA LEUCONEURA MASSANGEANA — prayer plant

This 16-inch plant is valued for its ornamental leaves. They are pale grayish-green with rose and brown and dark-green spots and silver markings. The plant needs an evenly moist soil and low or moderate light. Keep it out of direct sunlight. Beautiful under artificial light

Winter: Dry out between waterings. Moderate light.
Spring: Keep evenly moist. Moderate light.
Summer: Keep evenly moist. Low light.

MONSTERA DELICIOSA — Swiss cheese plant

Monstera is a climbing foliage plant to about 50 inches and has 24-inch perforated leaves. Grow it on a pole. Give it bright light and keep the soil evenly moist. Wash or wipe foliage about once a month. Older plants will bear unusual boat-shaped flowers. Don't let the aerial roots growing from the plant disturb you. They can be cut without harming the plant.

All Year: Follow fall schedule.

NEOREGELIA CAROLINAE — fingernail plant

This bromeliad with 30-inch rosette is a colorful spectacle for many months. The center turns brilliant red at bloom time. Give the plant bright light and keep the "vase" filled with water, the potting medium barely moist. Pot in equal parts of fir bark and soil.

Winter: Follow fall schedule.
Spring: Increase waterings somewhat. Sun.
Summer: Keep soil barely moist. Sun.

NICODEMIA DIVERSIFOLIA — indoor oak

A large plant that can grow to 60 inches, nicodemia has thin quilted leaves resembling an oak leaf. The foliage has a metallic green sheen. Give the plant a bright location and allow the soil to dry out between waterings. A splendid indoor tree.

All Year: Follow fall schedule.

NIDULARIUM INNOCENTII

An easy-to-grow bromeliad with colorful foliage and 20 to 24-inch rosettes. It is excellent for low light locations. Pot in equal parts of soil and fine-grade fir bark and keep evenly moist. As with most bromeliads, the "vase" should be kept filled with water.

All Year: Follow fall schedule.

ONCIDIUM ORNITHORYNCHUM

A lilac orchid with lovely sprays of flowers, this oncidium blooms in the fall. It is a 24-inch plant that requires good sunlight but likes cool growing conditions (60° F). Keep the potting medium evenly moist. Pot in fine-grade fir bark.

All Year: Follow fall schedule.

OPUNTIA BASILARIS — beaver-tail cactus

A plant with fleshy pads of bluish coppery color; *O. basilaris* grows to 40 inches. Needs full sun and even moisture. The beaver-tail cactus is very easy to grow but is hardly spectacular.

Winter: Grow almost dry. Sun.
Spring: Increase moisture. Sun.
Summer: Give plenty of water. Sun.

Maranta leuconeura massangeana

Monstera deliciosa

Neoregelia carolinae

Nicodemia diversifolia

Nidularium innocentii

Oncidium ornithorynchum

Opuntia basilaris

OPUNTIA MICRODASYS
bunny-ear cactus

The young pads of this 40-inch cacti resemble bunny's ears and hence the common name. Give this plant plenty of water and sun. An amenable indoor subject. Large specimens make fine decorator plants.

Winter: Grow almost dry. Sun.
Spring: Increase moisture. Sun.
Summer: Give plenty of water. Sun.

OSMANTHUS FRAGRANS
sweet olive

This 24-inch plant with plain green leaves and tiny white flowers is grown for its heady fragrance. Give it sun and keep soil evenly moist; only potbound plants bloom and prosper. Nice branching effect where mass is needed.

All Year: Follow fall schedule.

OXALIS HIRTA
wood sorrel

Weeds to some, flowers to others, oxalis blooms on and off throughout the year with pretty little violet flowers. Put four to six tubers in a 6-inch pot ½ inch deep in soil; keep fairly moist but don't overwater; increase waterings after growth starts. Give full sun. Rest for about two months at any time of year and then repot and resume growing.

See Chapter 7 for more information.

PENTAS LANCEOLATA
Egyptian star flower

The small rose flowers on this 30-inch plant provide a mass of color in winter. Grow in sun with plenty of water in active growth. Old plants get leggy, so every year start new ones from cuttings.

Winter: Grow somewhat dry. Sun.
Spring: Increase moisture. Sun.
Summer: Keep evenly moist. Bright light.

PEPEROMIA CAPERATA

A favorite terrarium plant, to 14 inches, with dark-green oval leaves, somewhat pendent in habit. Needs bright light and water sparingly. Good foliage plant for the beginner.

All Year: Follow fall schedule.

PEPEROMIA OBTUSIFOLIA

Perhaps the most popular small peperomia, this has rather large fleshy leaves. Plant grows lushly and likes plenty of water and bright light. Needs good air circulation to be at its best. Fine plant for terrariums.

Winter: Dry out between waterings. Bright light.
Spring: Follow fall schedule.
Summer: Follow fall schedule.

PEPEROMIA SANDERSII

A small 14-inch plant with dark-green leaves; good color. Undemanding and easy to grow. Needs only bright light; dry out between waterings. Not spectacular but certainly worth space. Fine for terrariums.

Winter: Dry out slightly. Bright light.
Spring: Follow fall schedule.
Summer: Follow fall schedule.

Opuntia microdasys

Osmanthus fragrans

Oxalis hirta

Pentas lanceolata

Peperomia caperata

Peperomia obtusifolia

Peperomia sandersii

PERESKIA ACULEATA
lemon vine

A cactus that has leaves, this 40-inch plant occasionally bears white or pink flowers in summer. It needs good sunlight; allow soil to dry out between waterings. Provide good air circulation. An unusual and pretty plant.

Winter: Follow fall schedule. Sun.
Spring: Follow fall schedule. Sun.
Summer: Keep evenly moist. Bright light.

POLYSCIAS BALFOURIANA
ming tree

An absolutely delightful 24-inch plant with frilly leaves; grow in low light locations and keep soil evenly moist. Not easy to grow but unusual and a challenge. Mature speciments make fine indoor trees.

Winter: Dry out between waterings. Low light.
Spring: Follow fall schedule. Moderate light.
Summer: Follow fall schedule. Moderate light.

POLYSCIAS FRUTICOSA

A 60-inch plant with very willowy branches and feathery leaves; quite handsome. Grow in low or moderate light and allow soil to dry out between waterings. Excellent indoor tree.

Winter: Dry out between waterings. Moderate light.
Spring: Follow fall schedule.
Summer: Follow fall schedule.

PORTEA PETROPOLITANA

A large 40-inch rosette, vase-shaped, and bearing a spectacular flower head — green and pink bracts. Needs excellent light to produce leaf color. Keep "vase" of plant filled with water and the growing medium — equal parts of fir bark and soil — somewhat dry.

All Year: Follow fall schedule.

PTERIS CRETICA 'WILSONII'
table fern

A 12-inch plant with slender green fronds, pteris likes a bright moist location with good air circulation. Give the plant sun in winter; keep soil evenly moist. Rapid grower under good conditions. Good dish garden and terrarium plant.

Winter: Keep soil evenly moist. Sun.
Spring: Provide ample water. Bright light.
Summer: Keep evenly moist. Bright light.

PTERIS TREMULA
Australian bracken

A fast-growing 24-inch fern with yellow-green fronds. Good for table decoration or window garden. Needs evenly moist soil and a bright place. Fine in a dish or terrarium.

All Year: Follow fall schedule.

PUNICA GRANATUM
pomegranate

Punica looks like a small tree, growing to 24 inches. It has tiny green leaves, sometimes red flowers. Give full sun and let soil dry out between waterings. Plant sheds leaves yearly so don't panic; it soon recovers.

Winter: Keep somewhat dry. Sun.
Spring: Increase moisture. Bright light.
Summer: Keep evenly moist. Bright light.

Pereskia aculeata

Polyscias balfouriana

Polyscias fruticosa

Portea petropolitana

Pteris cretica 'Wilsonii'

Pteris tremula

Punica granatum

REBUTIA KUPPERIANA

Don't overlook this tiny 2-inch cactus that bears 3-inch red flowers — it's quite a sight. Grow in sun; these desert denizens need more water than most cacti; grow somewhat dry and cool (60° F).

Winter: Keep almost moist. Sun.
Spring: Increase moisture. Sun.
Summer: Keep evenly moist. Sun.

REBUTIA MINUSCULA

If you have one rebutia, you will want more. This one is about 4 inches, a flattened globe with white spines. Bears scarlet blooms in bright sun. Keep well watered.

Winter: Keep almost moist. Sun.
Spring: Increase moisture. Sun.
Summer: Keep evenly moist. Sun.

REBUTIA VIOLACIFLORA

Perhaps the prettiest rebutia, this plant grows to 4 inches in diameter and bears magnificent purple flowers. Give it sun and grow it somewhat wet except in winter. Fine dish garden plant.

Winter: Keep almost moist. Sun.
Spring: Increase moisture. Sun.
Summer: Keep evenly moist. Sun.

RIVINA HUMILIS
rouge plant

Seldom grown but a delight is this 24-inch plant with drooping clusters of white flowers and red berries in fall and winter. Grow in sun with evenly moist soil. Excellent accent plant for tables.

All Year: Follow fall schedule.

ROHDEA JAPONICA

A fine 24-inch plant with stiff, dark, handsome leaves forming a rosette. Place in bright light and keep soil evenly moist. Slow growing, rohdea lives for years. Decorative red berries appear in fall. Excellent for growing under lights.

All Year: Follow fall schedule.

RUELLIA MAKOYANA

This 18-inch plant has beautiful silver-veined leaves and red flowers in winter — a treasured plant in my household. Grow in full sun and keep soil evenly moist. The plant is sensitive to overwatering.

Winter: Dry out between waterings. Bright light.
Spring: Keep evenly moist. Sun.
Summer: Provide plenty of water. Sun.

SAINTPAULIA
African violet

These small-to-medium plants need little introduction. They do bloom indoors profusely even in north light. They are sensitive to overwatering and prefer a very evenly moist soil. Drainage must be near perfect. Provide good air circulation too. Excellent for artificial light gardens.

Winter: Keep evenly moist. Sun.
Spring: Keep evenly moist. Bright light.
Summer: Dry out somewhat between waterings. Bright light.

Rebutia kupperiana

Rebutia minuscula

Rebutia violaciflora

Rivina humilis

Rohdea japonica

Ruellia makoyana

Saintpaulia

SELAGINELLA DRAUSSIANA

club moss

A 12-inch creeper with tiny bright-green leaves, this somewhat ferny plant will grow in low light. Soak soil and let dry out between waterings. Avoid water on leaves; it causes rot.

All Year: Follow fall schedule.

SELAGINELLA UNCINATA

With blue-green leaves, this 24-inch species is the one most often seen. It is somewhat branching, with tiny leaves, and looks like a miniature tree in time. Give it bright light and soak soil and allow to dry out between waterings.

All Year: Follow fall schedule.

SMITHIANTHA CINNABARINA

temple bells

A lovely 16-inch plant with serrated leaves and orange-red flowers. Start each rhizome in a 4 or 5-inch pot planting it 1 inch deep. Grow in sun and keep soil evenly moist. After plants bloom, store rhizome dry in pot in a cool shaded place for about three months. Then repot in fresh soil and place in light. Good under lights.

See Chapter 7 for more information.

SOLANDRA LONGIFLORA

cup-of-gold

A large vining plant, to 60 inches, with huge yellow-gold flowers. Needs plenty of space. It is difficult to grow: likes sun and an evenly moist soil. Mature plants will be able to adjust to indoor conditions; seedlings rarely do. For the adventurer.

Winter: Dry out between waterings. Sun.
Spring: Increase moisture. Sun.
Summer: Keep evenly moist. Bright light.

STRELITZIA REGINAE

bird-of-paradise

An exotic plant, to 48 inches, with orange flowers that resemble birds. The plant is difficult to grow under any conditions and refuses to bloom until it is at least five or six years old. Likes a bone-dry soil and then a thorough soaking; needs all the sun it can get. Try it if you like undertaking the near-impossible.

All Year: Follow fall schedule.

TIBOUCHINA SEMIDECANDRA

glory bush

A 30-inch outdoor plant that sometimes does very well indoors; it has magnificent purple flowers. The glory bush needs an almost wet soil and a bright location. It can grow into an impressive specimen, but takes care.

Winter: Dry out somewhat. Sun.
Spring: Increase moisture. Sun.
Summer: Provide plenty of water. Bright light.

ZYGOPETALUM MACKAYII

An exquisite 24-inch orchid with purple-brown and violet-blue flowers in fall. Plant in osmunda or fir bark and keep evenly moist; needs moderate or low light and good air circulation. Grow somewhat dry at this season until flower buds appear, and then increase moisture. Sometimes leaves get black streaks, but this doesn't harm the plant. Don't overwater.

Winter: Dry out severely. Bright light.
Spring: Increase waterings gradually. Bright light.
Summer: Keep evenly moist; then dry out. No sun.

Selaginella kraussiana

Selaginella uncinata

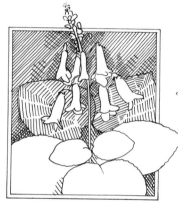

Smithiantha cinnabarina

Solandra longiflora

Strelitzia reginae

Tibouchina semidecandra

Zygopetalum mackayii

PART FOUR

WINTER

10 WINTER CARE AND DECORATION

In winter when the days are often dull and sunless, many plants grow slowly or not at all. This doesn't mean you should abandon them; they still need attention.

While plants are resting, gathering strength for new spring growth, soil should be kept barely moist but never completely dry. There's less light and cooler temperatures prevail in winter, so overwatering will kill plants. Instead of heavy watering, refresh plants with sprays of water lightly misted over foliage, and wash leaves to eliminate dust and soot. Plants that need repotting should be held over; don't repot now unless absolutely necessary.

Because plants are resting, they won't be sending out new growth — *don't* try to force plants into growth by feeding or you'll harm them. Even though the weather is cool, don't neglect good ventilation, because plants still need a fresh buoyant atmosphere. If windows can't be opened in the growing area, keep a small fan going to keep air moving.

If you use a lot of artificial heat, be sure to supply additional humidity with a small humidifier, or mist plants with water to compensate for the dry air. You can also place pots on pans full of gravel with some water; keep the pan filled to the gravel line with water. This will create some additional humidity, not much, but enough to get the plants through winter.

A general cleanup of the growing area to get ready for spring is certainly in order. This schedule includes scrubbing pots clean — a Brillo pad and boiling water do the job on clay pots — and making sure you have a supply of soil on hand for repotting in February and March. This is the time to rearrange plants to be sure sun lovers are in the right location and to put plants that like shade in a north exposure. As you move plants about for the new year you might want to discard plants that didn't adapt to your conditions. But before you do discard a plant, take a cutting to see if you can get a new plant growing.

Garden catalogs will be arriving in the mail, so now's a good time to decide whether you want to try some orchids or perhaps a few begonias. Take stock and see what you have and what you'll want for a new season of indoor gardening.

With rocks and stones, this dish garden relies on a single plant, plectranthus, for its beauty. Mosses and ferns cover the soil. (Photo by Matthew Barr)

Winter is the perfect time of the year to use small pots of orchids, bromeliads, begonias, and other flowering plants to brighten the house. Put plants on desks and tables for a week or so, but always return them to windows for light so they don't suffer too much in interior places. Use what you have to decorate indoor spots: the terrariums you made in autumn should be growing well, and some indoor bulbs you started in fall should be blooming.

DISH GARDENS

The phrase "dish garden" is used as a catch-all for an assortment of plants in a container. However, the dish garden is really a miniature landscape with small plants that duplicate a scene from nature. Similar to a terrarium, but not in an enclosed container, a dish garden offers much beauty for little work. Most important, however, it provides a tiny garden indoors when snow may be raging outdoors.

In the beginning, don't start with a grand composition; do something simple but well. Perhaps a woodland or desert landscape, or a hillside, meadow, seashore, or tropical scene.

When you choose the scene you want to make, it is wise to draw a pencil sketch — nothing elaborate, just symbols to indicate where each plant will be set into the scene. No matter which scene you do, try to use the elements of good design: proportion (each plant must relate to the other in mass and scale); balance (the entire scene must have balance); and scale (vertical and horizontal mass must be taken into consideration).

As with all crafts you will need some tools. The following are essential for dish gardens:

A small manicure scissors for pruning and trimming plants.

A small garden shears or bonsai pincette for trimming woody plants.

A pocketknife for cutting and pruning branches.

A single-edged razor blade for very fine detail work such as shaving barks and stems.

A trowel, flour scoop, or spoon to dig into soil.

Pliers for fashioning wire to train some plants.

A small hammer for breaking stones or pots.

Fine mesh hardware cloth to cover drainage holes in containers.

Copper wire to train branches.

Artist's brush to clean foliage.

Mister.

In the dish garden, as in bonsai, the container is part of the total picture you create and must blend with the overall composition.

The container can be a tray, a dish, a bowl, made of china or glass, ceramic or metal. Trays, dishes, and bowls come in many designs, shapes, and sizes, so take some time to make a selection. And don't overlook household items such as teacups and goblets, butter tubs and kegs, baking dishes and casseroles.

To start a dish garden, imbed rocks in the earth to simulate a natural landscape. (Photo by Matthew Barr)

Small plants are put in place and soil firmed around the collars of the plants. Here a miniature azalea is being planted. Note the ferny "tree" in the background. (Photo by Matthew Barr)

Here is the completed dish garden, a lovely winter garden that will last for months. (Photo by Matthew Barr)

Once you have the container be sure it is clean; wash and scrub it in hot water. Now, over the drainage holes (and do try to select containers with holes) lay a piece of fine mesh screen so soil will not sift out. Add a thin layer — about ¼ inch — of gravel with some charcoal chips to keep soil sweet. Put in a layer of soil to within ¼ inch of the top of the container.

Start to create your landscape by placing rocks or stones in position. Imbed the rocks or stones at least ¼ inch deep in the soil so they will appear natural and not as though they were placed there. A flat surface is uninteresting; hills and valleys can be made by contouring the soil with the palm of your hand.

Remove plants from their pots by tapping the side of the pot gently against a table edge. Crumble away a little soil from the root ball (not too much) and then dig small holes in the landscape for the plants. Insert the plants and firm the soil around the collar of each plant at the level it was in the pot.

Arrange the garden so that plants of different heights and different colors create an attractive picture. Use dark greens next to medium greens and never jump abruptly from dark plants to pale ones; this jars the eye. Remember to balance the scene using both vertical accents and horizontal lines. The plants must flow one into the other without abrupt voids.

167

A winter window of beautiful African violets; seasonal flowering plants such as cinerarias are in the background for more color. (Photo by Roche)

To finish the landscape you will want to use some sand or gravel or perhaps mosses to clothe the top of the soil. Sand and gravel go a long way toward creating a natural look, as do mosses and ground covers.

Water the garden slowly and gently. Never dump water; it will disrupt the soil and destroy the garden you have created. Place the dish in bright light near a window and inspect the scene from all angles. If you see a leaf or branch out of place, by all means cut it off. It will not harm the plant.

Plants in miniature gardens should not be fertilized; they will grow too rapidly. Use a rich soil with adequate nutrients. You also must select a soil that is porous to allow air and water to run through it (see Chapter 1).

The plants we suggest for miniature gardens are the same as the plants used for terrariums (see Chapter 7). Just what you select for your garden will depend on the scene you are creating. Of course plants like cacti and succulents are best suited for the desert landscape, while plants like begonias and calatheas are for tropical gardens. Refer to the seasonal plant descriptions.

11 GIFT PLANTS

WHEN SOMEONE gives you a gift plant, or if you buy one yourself, remember that it was growing under ideal conditions in greenhouses and was most likely forced into bloom for Thanksgiving or Christmas. You'll have to give your plant some extra attention at first. To keep the flowers as long as possible, place the plant in the coolest location in the home where there's moderate light. Never put it in the sun. The shock of transferral from the greenhouse into your home is severe, and cool temperatures and moderate light are what the plant needs to make the transition with as little harm as possible. Plants may lose a few leaves, but don't panic; just keep soil evenly moist and plants well groomed.

Place gift plants where they'll add the most color and provide the most cheer during the winter months. Try to find suitable places in a room — on a table or a desk where there is moderate light; or if it's a large plant, put it at floor level near a north window. The size of the plant will obviously dictate its placement; small plants like African violets or gloxinias can be at a north window, but a small azalea in full bloom or a beautiful Christmas cactus is better on a table or desk where it is always on display.

Once plants have finished blooming, let them dry out somewhat (this is the rest period they should have had in early winter but never did). Don't allow the soil to become bone-dry; keep it just moist to the touch. Don't feed the plant at all or you'll definitely kill it. Keep the plant as cool as possible for about a month, and then move it to slightly warmer temperatures. Still don't put the plant in sun; most gift plants for winter don't like sun at all. Increase watering in February, and as soon as new growth shows, apply a very weak solution of plant food (10-10-5).

One important thing I must mention is that many florists seem to be selling gift plants in a soil-less mix and are not telling people about it. (Of course, if the plant is a gift it would be hard to relay all information.) To see if you have a plant in a soil-less mix, poke your finger into it; if the medium is fluffy and almost like feathers and has no weight, you have a soil-less mix. This kind of mix requires feeding all the time, which is a chore, not a pleasure. In late February repot the plant in good rich soil so it will have natural nutrients from the soil rather than from chemical preparations.

Most gift plants come in terra cotta pots or plastic ones, usually wrapped in foil. Remove the foil immediately because it serves no purpose and is garish and useless. If you have a pretty cachepot or other elegant container of the right size, put the flower pot into the container; if you don't, a simple saucer will do.

Here are some of the popular gift plants and how to make them permanent residents:

Christmas Begonia

The Christmas begonia (*B. cheimantha*) is hard to grow because it tends to be temperamental and dislikes drafts and fluctuating temperatures. But it is worth trying to keep because it bears hundreds of pink flowers. Put the plant in a cool place to keep flowers for several weeks. Keep soil well watered (begonias like moisture). When the flowers fade, cut the plant back to about 6 inches and put it in warmth and bright light; soon new offshoots will start into growth. When the offshoots are about 3 or 4 inches tall, cut them from the mother plant and put them into a starter mix in shallow trays or pots. Cover the trays or pots with a Baggie to ensure good humidity. When roots form and plantlets are growing, put each one into rich soil in a 6-inch pot. Grow plantlets at a warm window where there is some sun. Now treat the begonia as you would a standard plant; good moisture, bright light, and even humidity; within a few months your new Christmas begonia will be in full leaf. Avoid fluctuating temperatures and drafts.

Cacti make fine gift plants any time of the year; this sculptured beauty is a cereus species. (Photo by Matthew Barr)

The floriferous Easter cactus is popular as a gift plant; its flowers are in shades of pink. Plants can be carried over from year to year. (Photo courtesy Johnson Cactus Gardens)

A new addition to the begonia family are the magnificently colored Rieger *elatior* types, which bloom over a very long period. These begonias need average home temperatures and evenly moist soil. They are much easier to grow than the Christmas begonias, but they do get quite spindly, so cut back after bloom time to keep the plants bushy and handsome. The Rieger begonias are available under various names. My plant is 'Aphrodite Cherry Red'; I got it in November and it bloomed on and off until May.

Euphorbia Splendens (crown-of-thorns)

This excellent indoor plant, with bright red flowers and handsome branching shape, grows easily without too much fuss. It needs a sandy soil and good bright light. The crown-of-thorns grows in coolness or warmth. Most plants are about 20 inches high when sold, but within a year or so they can reach 48 inches.

The crown-of-thorns grows into a treelike shape and needs judicious pruning now and then to make it look its best. The crown-of-thorns does have thorns which can prick the skin, so be careful when handling the plant. *E. splendens* is the true species, but many smaller varieties or improved types have been developed, including *E. splendens*. 'Bojeri' and a variety with yellow flowers. All seem to be amenable house plants that will be with you for some time, even with minimum care.

A lovely seasonal accent is the Christmas begonia, which is a bower of color in winter. New varieties of these old favorites are now available. (Photo courtesy Antonelli Bros.)

Gardenias (Cape jasmine)

Perseverance is the rule with gardenias. When buds show, start misting them with warm water, and keep misting them whenever you think about it. If you don't moisten the buds, they drop off or refuse to open, and you *do* want the scented small white flowers.

Put your gardenia in a cool (65°F) place where there is some sun. Give the plant bright light in summer and sun in winter, and be sure to keep humidity as high as possible. Feed with a fish fertilizer once a month in spring and summer, and soak the plant in a sink or pail of water once a month. If night temperature is above 70°F or below 60°F, buds may not open. The gardenia probably won't have too many flowers the first year, but it can adjust to new conditions after a while.

Red spider mites love gardenias, so get rid of insects immediately when you see them. Gardenias grow rapidly and become somewhat large; they look stunning in a white glazed tub.

Kalanchoes

Kalanchoes come in several colors, from red to orange to pink, in several varieties, but I still prefer the fiery red types derived from *K. blossfeldiana*. Make sure kalanchoes have a somewhat sandy soil, and always keep it moist. Give the plants bright light; sun is not necessary. Leaves are closely crowded together, so watch for any insects. (I spray leaves with water to flush off any egg insects.)

Kalanchoes bloom at Christmas, but if you cut away faded flowers in February, plants will bear another crop of blooms in April, a definite bonus.

Orchids (cattleyas)

Cattleyas are hard to grow indoors, but not impossible. These gems come in almost every color but blue or black, and every size from 2 to 10 inches in diameter. Some cattleyas bloom twice a year, with regal and dramatic flowers that last for four to six weeks if plants are kept in a cool place.

The crucial time for cattleyas is after bloom, so remove faded flowers and then water the plant only once every ten days for about three months, or until new growth starts. Repot the plant at the first sign of new growth, being careful not to break the growing point. Put the plant into fir bark, *never* in soil. Water the bark lightly until the

Cattleyas are well known as corsage flowers; mature plants are inexpensive and can be with you for years. They come in an array of lovely colors. (Photo by Joyce R. Wilson)

plant has established itself (one month or so), and then resume regular waterings twice a week or more. Make sure cattleyas have plenty of sun and warmth, and provide cool temperatures at night. Some of my cattleyas have bloomed faithfully for years; in fact, the first plant I ever grew twenty years ago was a cattleya.

Poinsettias

Today white, pink, and greenish-yellow poinsettias compete with the traditional red plant. Poinsettias can be difficult to grow-on; the secret is coolness — plants need temperatures of about 50 to 55°F to prosper, which aren't easy to maintain in most homes. Keep soil evenly moist, and give plants good bright light (sunlight can harm plants). Cut back the plant in early spring and put it outside on a porch or in the garden. When fall comes, bring the plant indoors and increase watering until November. In November, grow the poinsettia somewhat dry and put it in a dark place at night (where no artificial light gets to it) for about five weeks to encourage blooming in winter.

There are also dwarf poinsettias. The variety 'Mikkelson' is more robust and more floriferous than the standard plants. The dwarfs are easier to grow than the standard poinsettias, and their color lasts for months.

Zygocactus

The Christmas cactus, Easter cactus, and Thanksgiving cactus have an array of botanical names, including zygocactus (Christmas or Thanksgiving), and schlumbergera (Easter). One year I got a so-called Christmas cactus; it was really a Thanksgiving one. Another year I discovered that my Easter cactus was really a Christmas one. So don't worry about the botanical names of these plants.

Zygocactus, the traditional Christmas cactus, is a low-growing, rather pendent plant, with pink to brick-red flowers on the tips of the leaves. The scalloped green leaves somewhat resemble a crab's claw. You'll have to follow some stringent rules if you want plants to thrive. Most cacti grow in the desert, but zygocactus naturally grows in shady and moist rain forests. The plants like good air circulation, bright light, ample moisture, and need a somewhat different soil mix than most plants. Because zygocacti are air plants, they don't like their roots smothered in soil; they prefer an equal mixture of fir bark and soil. Average home temperatures are fine all year.

To make your cactus bloom, in September put it in a dark place, because any artificial light whatsoever will inhibit or completely curtail bud formation. Keep the plant there for six to eight weeks, and water it. Once buds show, move the plant to a bright area for bloom. If you have an Easter cactus, start the dark-inhibition period six to eight weeks prior to Easter; start a Thanksgiving cactus six to eight weeks before that holiday. Normally these plants are rarely bothered by pests of any type and respond well to routine culture.

12 WHAT TO DO IN WINTER

BEGONIAS

Some begonias are still growing in the dull months but the majority have passed their peak and need very little care.

Water and Light: Reduce moisture to about once a week; keep soil just barely moist and provide a very airy light place for all begonias. Keep plants in sun or bright light.

Temperature and Humidity: Excessive artificial heat desiccates begonias so provide additional moisture in the air. A space humidifier will supply this. Keep good ventilation; open a window a crack so air can reach plants, but be sure no begonia is in a draft or near a hot air register or radiator.

Feeding: Stop all feeding. Plants do not need it. Many begonias rest in winter. This is a good time to prune and trim and shape plants. Don't do any severe pruning until spring, though. Just concentrate on keeping them neat.

Note: Begonias — especially the rhizomatous and hairy-leaved ones — make fine desk or table accents, so use them around the house for decoration. Return them to bright light after a week or so; longer periods away from light can harm them.

BROMELIADS

In the gray days of winter you can enjoy the colorful leaves and lush growth of bromeliads. Many are in bloom now. Six bromeliads can make any winter window a bright garden.

Water and Light: Keep plants in the best possible light — sun is preferable. If you cannot provide natural light you might want to use artificial lamps. Even a single lamp will supply some light for the plants. Keep growing medium moist at all times.

Temperature and Humidity: Keep bromeliads in temperate conditions; never let temperatures go below 68°F in the growing area and mist plants frequently. Rooms are apt to be very dry from artificial heating in these months.

Feeding: Do not feed plants at all.

BULBS

As in fall, the early part of winter is still a time to start bulbs and many can be planted in pots for spring bloom (some bloom into early summer). Both one-season bulbs and all-year types can be started now.

Water and Light: Some of the bulbs started in fall will need somewhat more water now; even moisture is best and plants should be brought into light. Those just started require fall treatment (see fall section).

Temperature and Humidity: Both temperature and humidity requirements depend on the bulb being grown. Generally, coolness (60°F) is best and humidity should be about 30 percent. See Chapter 7.

Feeding: No feeding necessary.

CACTI

Gardeners dispute whether cacti should be rested completely dry during this season or whether they should continue to be watered. I opt to keep them barely moist, watering plants in 4 or 5-inch pots about once every two weeks.

Water and Light: Keep soil barely moist, almost on the dry side, and place plants in a bright or sunny location.

Temperature and Humidity: Move cacti to a somewhat cool place, an unheated pantry or other cool storage area where temperatures are about 65°F. This suits them as they start their rest. Exceptions would be some of the rebutias, which are winter-blooming; these require the same treatment as in summer.

Feeding: Avoid feeding any cacti during the winter.

FERNS

Because of the pendent growth of most ferns it is a good idea to grow them as hanging plants; they are lovely at eye level and fronds have ample space to grow without hitting windows or furniture. Like palms, ferns need little attention in the winter.

Water and Light: Keep the soil barely moist and the plants in a cool bright place. Too much tender loving care does more harm now than good.

Temperature and Humidity: Keep plants in a somewhat cool place. Mist area around plants or set pots on moist gravel to provide additional humidity.

Feeding: Do not feed plants at all.

GERANIUMS

Use geraniums to bring color to winter windows. Keep plants groomed and tidy.

Water and Light: Keep soil evenly moist; geraniums have no dormant period; this is the time to give geraniums full sun. Indeed, they need it if they are to prosper in the following year. If light is minimal consider using artificial lamps for the plants.

Temperature and Humidity: In winter it is important to provide a free flow of air for the plants. Stagnant conditions should be avoided. Keep geraniums as cool as possible.

Feeding: No feeding necessary now.

GESNERIADS

Most gesneriads have finished blooming, but African violets are in full color and very pretty. Even in shade they will bear some flowers.

Water and Light: In general, keep gesneriads evenly moist through winter. Keep them in a light place; in fact some sunlight is very beneficial during the winter months.

Temperature and Humidity: Try to place plants where temperatures are somewhat moderate, about 68°F. Maintain average humidity of 20 percent. Too much moisture in the air coupled with dark days can encourage fungous disease.

Feeding: If you have been feeding plants, stop and allow them to grown naturally through winter, when many gesneriads take a rest.

FLOWERING PLANTS

Some flowers will still be showing but generally this is a quiet time for most flowering plants.

Water and Light: Keep soil just barely moist — water plants and then allow them to dry out before watering again. Light outside is hardly intense, so plants can be in bright or sunny light.

Temperature and Humidity: If you keep your house cool now (65°F) to save fuel, this is fine for plants too. They tolerate coolness when not actively growing. However, still mist plants occasionally when days are sunny to provide additional moisture in the air.

Feeding: In general, discontinue feeding flowering plants now; exceptions would be the few that are still blooming.

FOLIAGE PLANTS

Winter is the time to enjoy your foliage plants to the fullest as green accents indoors. Most (if you have followed the seasonal suggestions) should be in peak form.

Water and Light: Continue the fall schedule; that is, allow plant soil to dry out between waterings and be sure plants are in good bright light. Some sun is fine.

Temperature and Humidity: No special care needed; maintain average home temperature and humidity. Mist plants frequently if you use a great deal of artificial heat in the home.

Feeding: Some light feeding — about once a month — will not kill plants, but generally discontinue plant foods through the winter.

ORCHIDS

Many orchids are blooming now with bright flowers, furnishing distinctive decoration for the winter months. Bright blooms of masdevallias and coelogynes and other orchids look especially handsome.

Water and Light: The orchids that bloomed in summer should now have a rest, three to four weeks with just a little water; but those coming into bloom should have ample water. As soon as you see spikes growing, increase moisture and light. Indeed, almost any orchid will benefit from winter sun, so do move plants around a bit. (See seasonal plant descriptions for individual orchid care.)

Temperature and Humidity: Too much moisture in the air at this time of year can be detrimental to the plants if days are very cloudy. Fungus will be the result, so put away the misting bottle.

Feeding: Do not feed any orchids now; let them grow on their own.

Note: This is the time when I cut many sprays of orchids for Christmas decoration. It is a welcome change from poinsettias. Put cut orchids in a vase of water; they will last for several weeks.

PALMS

During winter, palms take care of themselves and need very little care. They are recuperating from spring growth. Don't smother them with attention.

Water and Light: Keep soil barely moist and plants in a bright place; be careful not to overwater plants at this time of year. It will do far more harm than good.

Temperature and Humidity: Average home temperatures are fine for palms, and some coolness at night very beneficial for them. Humidity may naturally be low indoors now because artificial heat takes the moisture out of the air, so misting is helpful.

Feeding: Do not feed palms in winter; let them have their quiet period. You can, however, trim away errant fronds and shape and trim palms somewhat as winter comes to a close.

SUCCULENTS

If you are busy with the holidays you can forget your succulent plants because they almost take care of themselves now. And generally, although they don't have a complete rest, there is little growth.

Water and Light: Keep soil just barely moist; in other words if you were watering twice a week in autumn (depending on pot size) now reduce watering to once a week. Keep plants in sun or bright light; either exposure is fine now.

Temperature and Humidity: While succulents can tolerate wide varieties of temperatures if necessary, do not subject them to intense cold conditions and also avoid a stuffy hot atmosphere. Because artificial heat dries out plants, keep humidity at a safe level — 20 percent is all right and 30 percent is better.

Feeding: Do not feed at this time of year. It can upset the biorhythm of the plant.

HOUSE PLANTS FOR WINTER

ACORUS GRAMINEUS   sweet flag
This small grassy-leaved plant grows to 10 inches and is a lovely green accent indoors. The sweet flag grows in bright light (or less if necessary) and needs buckets of water to prosper. Keep the soil almost wet.
Spring: Keep soil evenly moist. Moderate light.
Summer: Follow winter schedule.
Fall: Follow winter schedule.

AECHMEA ANGUSTIFOLIA
This vase-shaped bromeliad grows to 30 inches, with decorative leaves and a flower head crowded with tiny blooms. The plant likes bright light. Fill the "vase" with water and keep the potting medium just barely moist.
Spring: Increase moisture somewhat. Sun.
Summer: Provide plenty of water. Sun.
Fall: Keep soil evenly moist. Sun.

AECHMEA RACINAE   Christmas bromeliad
A. racinae is a fine bromeliad that grows to 10 inches; it has green leaves and a distinctive flower scape of red berrylike flowers edged black. Needs bright light; keep the fir-bark-and-soil mix evenly moist. The flowers last a month.
Spring: Follow winter schedule.
Summer: Increase water somewhat. Bright light.
Fall: Keep soil evenly moist. Bright light.

AGAVE FILIFERA
This is a dense rosette, growing to 20 inches; the leaves are spiny and decorated with tiny threads. Give it sun and keep soil just evenly moist. *A. filifera* can tolerate abuse if necessary and still look handsome.
Spring: Increase waterings. Sun.
Summer: Provide plenty of water. Sun.
Fall: Keep soil evenly moist. Sun.

AGAVE VICTORIAE REGINAE   century plant
This 10-inch rosette of olive leaves penciled white is a compact globe of beauty that looks like a piece of jade. It needs sun, and soil that is just barely moist. Keep it very cool in winter. A stunning succulent.
Spring: Increase waterings somewhat. Sun.
Summer: Keep evenly moist. Sun.
Fall: Dry out between waterings. Sun.

AGLAONEMA COMMUTATUM   Chinese evergreen
A popular 24-inch plant with dark-green leaves marked with silver. Easy to grow; takes sun or low light. Keep soil evenly moist.
All Year: Follow winter schedule.

ALLIUM NEAPOLITANUM   flowering onion
Don't let the common name throw you. This is a beautiful bulbous plant, to 30 inches, with slender leaves and crowns of white flowers. Alliums started in fall require bright light and cool (60° F) conditions. Give plenty of water. After blooms fade, dry off plant somewhat and place in coolness (55° F) for a few months; then repot and start watering again.
See Chapter 7 for more information.

Acorus gramineus

Aechmea angustifolia

Aechmea racinae

Agave filifera

Agave victoriae reginae

Aglaonema commutatum

Allium neapolitanum

ALOE ARISTATA
lace aloe

Only 6 inches in diameter, *A. aristata* is a gray-green rosette dotted white and tipped with white marginal teeth. Give the plant sun and a sandy well-drained soil. Keep barely moist; a saturated condition will kill it. Spectacular yellow or orange flowers in fall or winter if grown in a very sunny place.

Spring: Increase waterings somewhat. Sun.
Summer: Keep evenly moist. Sun.
Fall: Dry out between watering. Bright light.

ALOE VERA

A rather ungainly plant, hardly attractive, this 10-inch gray-green rosette has gained popularity because its milky juices heal burns. The plant needs sun and an evenly moist soil. It's more a curiosity than a decorative plant, but grow it if its healing powers intrigue you.

Spring: Increase waterings. Sun.
Summer: Keep evenly moist. Sun.
Fall: Dry out between waterings. Bright light.

ANTHURIUM SCHERZERIANUM
flamingo flower

Here is a plant with striking foliage and in winter some lovely lacquered-red flowers. The 20-inch flamingo flower needs a rich soil kept moist. High humidity (60 percent) is required, and the plant does best in low light. Difficult to grow but very exotic in bloom.

Spring: Keep quite moist. Low light.
Summer: Provide plenty of water. Low light.
Fall: Keep evenly moist. Low light.

ARAUCARIA EXCELSA
Norfolk Island pine

A green-needled 48 to 60-inch plant, *A. excelsa* is an excellent house plant. It requires bright light and an evenly moist soil. And while it is slow-growing, it is certainly dependable and will be with you for many years.

Spring: Follow winter schedule.
Summer: Increase water somewhat. Bright light.
Fall: Follow winter schedule.

ARDISIA CRENATA
coralberry

This colorful Christmas plant looks somewhat like a little holly tree. It grows to about 24 inches and the fragrant white flowers are followed by long-lasting coral-red or white berries. The plant needs bright light and a soil that is just moist. Occasionally, give it a deep soaking in a pail of water.

Spring: Keep soil evenly moist. Sun.
Summer: Keep soil evenly moist. Bright light.
Fall: Dry out slightly. Bright light.

ARTHROPODIUM CIRRHINATUM

Here is a lily that grows to 36 inches. It has light-green grassy leaves and clusters of starry white flowers in January and February. Give it plenty of sun and copious water during active growth and bloom. Decrease the moisture after flowering, but never allow the soil to dry out completely.
See Chapter 7 for more information.

ASPARAGUS SPRENGERI
emerald fern

This lovely lacy plant is very popular and can reach 48 inches across. It is an exceptionally good indoor plant with needlelike foliage; in winter after small flowers appear, red berries are an additional bonus. For best results give it bright light and plenty of water.

All Year: Follow winter schedule.

Aloe aristata

Aloe vera

Anthurium scherzerianum

Araucaria excelsa

Ardisia crenata

Arthropodium cirrhinatum

Asparagus sprengeri

AUCUBA JAPONICA GOLDIEANA   gold dust tree

A fine 40 to 50-inch plant with yellow-spotted foliage; very handsome. The plant needs low or moderate light and plenty of water. Good indoor tree.

Spring: Keep evenly moist. Moderate light.
Summer: Keep evenly moist. Moderate light.
Fall: Dry out between waterings. Some sun.

AZALEA

These are popular gift plants for Christmas and the miniature or dwarf varieties are especially suitable for indoors. Flowers may be white, pink, or red, and are a mass of color for the gray winter months. To keep azaleas as long as possible, provide a cool place (60° F) and keep them out of sunlight.

Spring: Cut back at end of spring; repot and put in bright light in garden.
Summer: Water heavily. Bright light.
Fall: Return to house; keep soil evenly moist. Bright light.

BEGONIA BOWERI   eyelash begonia

This is a lovely 14-inch begonia with delicate green leaves edged black, and pink flowers. Give it bright light and let soil dry out thoroughly between waterings. The plant may rest in very late winter; water sparingly through these weeks until you see signs of new growth. Excellent for light gardens; good in terrariums.

Spring: Increase waterings. Sun.
Summer: Keep evenly moist. Bright light.
Fall: Keep evenly moist. Bright light.

BEGONIA CHEIMANTHA   Christmas begonia

This is one of the most difficult begonias to grow. It is a 30-inch plant that is covered with pink or red flowers in the winter. It needs cool (60° F) growing conditions and must be in a draft-free bright place, with the soil kept constantly wet but never soggy.
See Chapter 11 for more information.

BEGONIA HERACIFOLIA   star begonia

This plant grows to about 20 inches, with star-shaped leaves and pink flowers. It is a rhizomatous begonia and needs bright light; allow soil to dry out between waterings. Good under artificial light.

Spring: Increase waterings. Bright light.
Summer: Keep soil evenly moist. Bright light.
Fall: Reduce water somewhat. Sun.

BEGONIA LIMMINGHEIANA

A trailing begonia to about 40 inches, this is a beautiful plant in bloom with masses of flowers. It requires bright light and evenly moist soil. One of the prettiest basket begonias, but somewhat difficult to grow.

Spring: Follow winter schedule. Bright light.
Summer: Keep evenly moist. Bright light.
Fall: Keep evenly moist. Sun.

BILLBERGIA NUTANS   queen's tears

Growing to 30 inches and with grassy green foliage, queen's tears bear chartreuse, pink, and cerise flowers in midwinter; an exquisite display of color. Unlike most bromeliads, these do not have a vase shape, but rather grassy leaves. Grow the plant in moderate or low light and keep the soil quite moist. Pot in medium-grade fir bark.

All Year: Follow winter schedule.

Aucuba japonica goldieana

Azalea

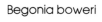

Begonia boweri

Begonia cheimantha

Begonia heracifolia

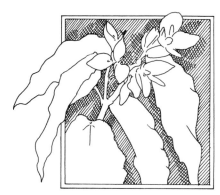

Begonia limmingheiana

Billbergia nutans

CARISSA GRANDIFLORA
Natal plum

This spiny, but not thorny, vining shrub grows to about 30 inches indoors and has lovely small glossy green leaves and scented white flowers, followed by red berries in winter. It needs full sun and an evenly moist soil. Mature plants make fine indoor trees.

Spring: Keep evenly moist. Sun.
Summer: Keep evenly moist. Sun.
Fall: Dry out between waterings. Bright light.

CEROPEGIA WOODII
string-of-hearts

A popular vine that grows to 20 inches, the string-of-hearts has heart-shaped leaves and pink or purple blooms at the ends of trailing stems. A very unusual plant. Give it full sun and let soil dry out between waterings.

Spring: Keep soil evenly moist. Sun.
Summer: Keep soil evenly moist. Bright light.
Fall: Dry out between waterings. Sun.

CHLOROPHYTUM ELATUM
spider plant

This 30 to 40-inch branching, grassy-leaved plant is a delight. Grows easily because it has its own water storage tubers in case you forget it. The spider plant grows in bright or moderate light with lots of water or little water. It is certainly a plant for those who think they can't grow anything.

Spring: Keep evenly moist. Moderate or low light.
Summer: Keep evenly moist. Moderate or low light.
Fall: Dry out between waterings. Bright light.

CHRYSALIDOCARPUS LUTESCENS
fan palm

This beautiful palm, sometimes called areca, grows to about 40 inches and has branching fronds. It requires moderate or low light and evenly moist soil. Try it if you have a room corner where you need a green accent during the dull winter months.

All Year: Follow winter schedule.

COELOGYNE CRISTATA

A 20-inch orchid with rather grassy leaves and 3-inch crystal-white dazzling flowers in January and February. For all its beauty it is not easy to grow and requires some special tricks. Grow it moderately moist all year until October. Then water it only about once a week and keep it in sun to encourage flower buds. When buds appear, increase moisture and continue to water it regularly while it blooms. After flowering, carry it almost bone-dry for at least five to six weeks, then resume watering so new foliage can develop. Grow in fine-grade fir bark.

COFFEA ARABICA
coffee plant

This evergreen shrub will grow to about 40 inches and is handsome winter decoration with its glossy green leaves and red berries. Give the coffee plant bright light and keep the soil almost wet. It likes a lot of water.

Spring: Keep soil evenly moist. Sun.
Summer: Keep soil evenly moist. Bright light.
Fall: Dry out somewhat between waterings. Sun.

COLOCASIA ESCULENTA
elephant-ears

True to its common name, this plant has huge leaves and grows to about 48 inches. It is elegant-looking, and needs bright light and heavy water while in growth in early summer. Start tubers, two to an 8-inch pot, in spring; they will be at their peak in summer. Reduce moisture in fall, and in winter when plants are dormant, carry them dry in pots at 55° F.

Carissa grandiflora

Ceropegia woodii

Chlorophytum elatum

Chrysalidocarpus lutescens

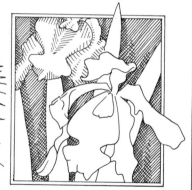

Coelogyne cristata

Coffea arabica

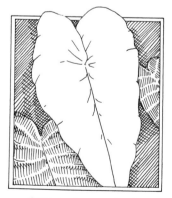

Colocasia esculenta

CYCLAMEN

If you have cool conditions (60° F), cyclamens can be colorful all winter. Put them in a bright location and water them almost every day. The pretty dark-green mottled leaves are heart-shaped; the flowers are dazzling and come in many colors. To carry them over, when flowers fade, let the plant rest by gradually withholding water until foliage dies. Keep nearly dry, the pot on its side, in a shaded place, perhaps an unheated garage or pantry where it is cool (about 50° F), until August or early September. Then remove dead foliage and repot in fresh soil. Set the top of the tuber level with the surface of the soil; otherwise water may collect in the depression and cause crown rot.
See Chapter 7 for more information.

CYPERUS ALTERNIFOLIUS

This tall 30-inch plant has erect stems crowned with a fountain of leaves. It grows best in low or moderate light and needs buckets of water. (It is naturally a water plant.) If you want something different, try this one.

All Year: Follow winter schedule.

DAPHNE ODORA
fragrant daphne

This 30-inch plant has lovely green leaves and whitish pink flowers, highly scented. It requires cool conditions (60° F) and some sun. Keep the soil evenly moist. It's a difficult plant to grow but worth the trouble because it has such lovely fragrance.

Spring: Keep evenly moist. Sun.
Summer: Keep evenly moist. Bright light.
Fall: Dry out between waterings. Bright light.

DRACAENA FRAGRANS
corn plant

A popular 36-inch plant with leaves that are edged in yellow. The plant needs good light, not sun, and soil should be kept evenly moist. Don't let water accumulate on leaves; it can cause spotting.

Spring: Follow winter schedule. Bright light.
Summer: Increase waterings. Bright light.
Fall: Keep evenly moist. Sun.

DRACAENA GODSEFFIANA

This variegated dracaena with large yellow and green leaves grows to 30 inches. The plant needs bright light; allow soil to dry out between waterings.

Spring: Keep soil evenly moist. Bright light.
Summer: Keep soil evenly moist. Bright light.
Fall: Dry out between waterings. Sun.

DRACAENA MARGINATA
dragon plant

A popular decorator plant, *D. marginata* grows to 48 inches with a lovely branching habit and narrow green leaves edged red. It grows in moderate or low light; allow soil to dry out between waterings.

Spring: Keep evenly moist. Moderate light.
Summer: Provide ample moisture. Moderate light.
Fall: Allow soil to dry out between waterings. Moderate light.

DRACAENA SANDERIANA

This 20-inch plant has green leaves banded white and makes a handsome indoor accent. Like most dracaenas, it needs bright light but little if any sun; allow soil to dry out between waterings.

Spring: Keep soil evenly moist. Bright light.
Summer: Provide ample moisture. No sun.
Fall: Dry out between waterings. Bright light.

Cyclamen

Cyperus alternifolius

Daphne odora

Dracaena fragrans

Dracaena godseffiana

Dracaena marginata

Dracaena sanderiana

DRACAENA WARNECKII

A lovely 24-inch rosette of green leaves striped white, this dracaena is perhaps the most popular in the group. It needs bright light; allow the soil to dry out between waterings. Excellent decorator plant.

Spring: Keep soil evenly moist. Bright light.
Summer: Provide ample moisture. No sun.
Fall: Dry out between waterings. Bright light.

EUPHORBIA PULCHERRIMA   poinsettia

Traditionally known as the Christmas flower, this 40-inch plant with lobed leaves and red bracts is highly popular. When you buy it or receive it put it in a sunny but cool window (60° F). Water every other day until leaves start to fall. Then reduce moisture until the soil is almost dry, and put the plant in a shady window (at about 55° F). Water it about once a month.
See Chapter 11 for yearly care schedule.

EUPHORBIA SPLENDENS   crown-of-thorns

This handsome 40-inch branching plant with small green leaves and red flowers is a desirable addition to winter gardens. It does best in sunlight; allow the soil to dry out between waterings. The crown-of-thorns makes a handsome room plant but do be careful when handling; the thorns are sharp and can cut.
See Chapter 11 for yearly care schedule.

GREVILLEA ROBUSTA   silk oak

This is a fast-growing plant to about 40 inches with delicate foliage. It almost takes care of itself. Give it some sunlight and ample water. An unusual treelike plant.

Spring: Follow winter schedule.
Summer: Provide ample moisture. Bright light.
Fall: Keep soil evenly moist. Sun.

GYNURA AURANTIACA   purple velvet plant

Here is a popular 30-inch ornamental plant with large purple leaves. It requires bright or moderate light and ample moisture. The foliage almost glows with color. Pretty in baskets.

Spring: Keep soil evenly moist. Bright light.
Summer: Keep soil evenly moist. Moderate light.
Fall: Dry out soil between waterings. Bright light.

GYNURA SARMENTOSA

Similar to *G. aurantiaca*, this plant has lobed leaves, highly colored in purple and green, and grows to 36 inches. It is a vinelike plant that requires a bright place but no sun. Provide ample moisture. Nice basket plant.

Spring: Keep soil evenly moist. Bright light.
Summer: Keep soil evenly moist. Moderate light.
Fall: Keep soil barely moist. Bright light.

HOFFMANNIA GHEISBREGHTII

A splendid 30-inch foliage plant with velvety brown-green leaves tinged with red. It grows well in bright or low light; keep soil evenly moist. An excellent plant wherever a bright accent is needed.

All Year: Follow winter schedule.

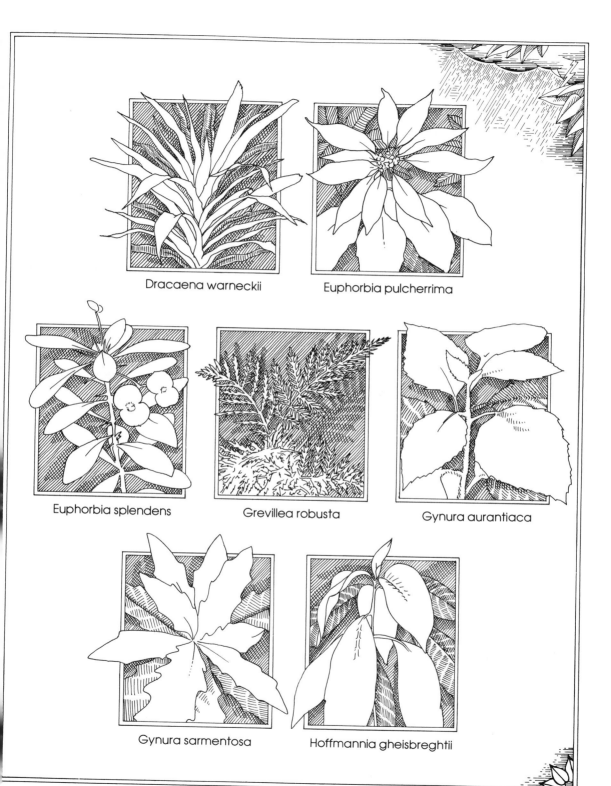

Dracaena warneckii

Euphorbia pulcherrima

Euphorbia splendens

Grevillea robusta

Gynura aurantiaca

Gynura sarmentosa

Hoffmannia gheisbreghtii

HOFFMANNIA REFULGENS

Smaller than *H. gheisbreghtii*, this hoffmannia has dark-green leaves edged with magenta and rose. Place it in a bright location; allow soil to dry out between waterings.

Spring: Keep soil evenly moist. Bright light.
Summer: Keep soil evenly moist. Moderate light.
Fall: Dry out between waterings. Bright light.

HOFFMANNIA ROEZLII

With copper-brown and brown foliage, this 30-inch plant is highly desirable because of its lovely color. It needs bright light and evenly moist soil.

Spring: Follow winter schedule. Bright light.
Summer: Increase waterings. Moderate light.
Fall: Keep soil evenly moist. Bright light.

KALANCHOE BLOSSFELDIANA

Very popular as a Christmas plant, this kalanchoe has small succulent green leaves and tiny bright red flowers, making a bower of color at Christmas time. It needs coolness (65° F) and a bright place. Allow the soil to dry out between waterings. If you grow this kalanchoe with care there will be a second crop of flowers in early spring.

Spring: Keep soil evenly moist. Sun.
Summer: Keep soil evenly moist. Bright light.
Fall: Dry out between waterings. Sun.

KALANCHOE TOMENTOSA   panda plant

Grown for its lovely foliage, this 20-inch plant has brown-spotted gray-green fuzzy leaves and is charming. It will need a bright location. Allow the soil to dry out well between waterings. Be sure not to overwater or rot may occur.

Spring: Increase waterings. Bright light.
Summer: Keep soil evenly moist. Moderate light.
Fall: Dry out between waterings. Bright light.

LANTANA CAMARA

A shrubby spreading plant to 20 inches, *L. camara* bears orange flowers, very pretty in winter. It needs sun. After flowering, cut back the plant and grow somewhat dry. Then when you see fresh growth repot in new soil.

Spring: Increase moisture. Sun.
Summer: Keep soil very moist. Sun.
Fall: Keep soil evenly moist. Bright light.

LANTANA MONTEVIDENSIS

This trailer to 36 inches has small clusters of lavender flowers in the dead of winter. It does need a bright sunny place and ample moisture. It revels in coolness (55° F) and is a very fine indoor plant. Splendid for basket growing.

Spring: Follow winter schedule. Sun.
Summer: Provide ample water. Sun.
Fall: Dry out between waterings. Sun.

LICUALA GRANDIS

Little known but lovely, this palm grows to about 48 inches and has wide foliage fans. It thrives in almost any light situation — shade or sun — and likes plenty of water now.

Spring: Keep soil evenly moist. Bright light.
Summer: Provide ample moisture. No sun.
Fall: Keep soil evenly moist. Bright light.

Hoffmannia refulgens

Hoffmannia roezlii

Kalanchoe blossfeldiana

Kalanchoe tomentosa

Lantana camara

Lantana montevidensis

Licuala grandis

LOBIVIA AUREA

A 4-inch globular cactus, ribbed and with spines, *L. aurea* bears lemon-yellow flowers if grown in sun. The plant needs even moisture and makes a fine subject for beginners.

Spring: Keep soil evenly moist. Sun.
Summer: Provide ample moisture. Sun.
Fall: Dry out between waterings. Sun.

LYCORIS RADIATA   hardy amaryllis

A deciduous bulbous plant from China, lycoris grows to 48 inches. It bears large flowers in this season. Start bulbs with nose just above the soil, one to a 7-inch pot, in April or May. Water moderately until the end of summer; then flood plant. Move to a sunny place. As leaf growth develops in late fall, flowers appear. In spring, store the plant.
See Chapter 7 for more information.

LYGODIUM JAPONICUM   climbing fern

A vining plant to 40 inches, lygodium has light lacy blue-green fronds, very attractive. The plant likes moderate or low light with a little sun in spring and winter. Keep the soil evenly moist. An unusual fern and one worth growing.

Spring: Follow winter schedule.
Summer: Keep soil evenly moist. Low light.
Fall: Keep soil evenly moist. Moderate light.

MAMMILLARIA HAHNIANA   pincushion cactus

A 10 to 14-inch globe cactus with curly white hairs and fine red flowers in winter. This desert plant is easily grown in a bright window, with water every other week.

Spring: Increase moisture. Sun.
Summer: Provide ample water. Sun.
Fall: Dry out between waterings. Bright light.

MAMMILLARIA RHODANTHA

A somewhat large 20-inch spiny globe, this one is for true cactus lovers. It needs bright light; allow soil to dry out between waterings.

Spring: Increase moisture. Sun.
Summer: Provide ample water. Sun.
Fall: Dry out between waterings. Bright light.

MANETTIA INFLATA   Mexican firecracker

A climbing plant to 24 inches, with tubular yellow-tipped red flowers that bloom on and off through the winter months. Give manettia bright light and let the soil dry out between waterings. This one thrives when potbound, so repot as seldom as possible; requires an airy location.

All Year: Follow winter schedule.

MASDEVALLIA IGNEA

A showy orchid, *M. ignea* has very large red flowers and blooms in winter. It likes coolness and will need bright light; keep potting medium moist all year.

All Year: Follow winter schedule.

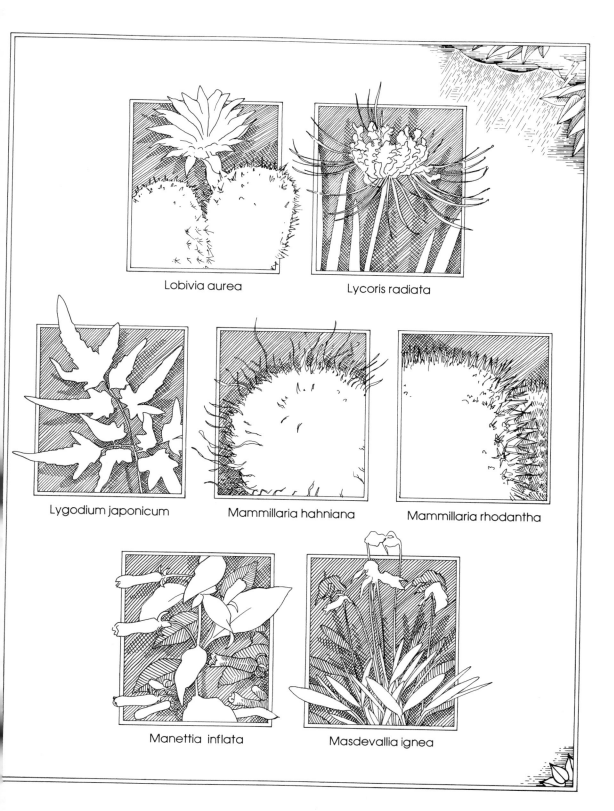

Lobivia aurea

Lycoris radiata

Lygodium japonicum

Mammillaria hahniana

Mammillaria rhodantha

Manettia inflata

Masdevallia ignea

MEDINILLA MAGNIFICA

love plant

A lush blue-green plant to 40 inches, with stunning panicles of carmine flowers and tiny pink bracts. Blossoming can occur any time of the year, but generally in winter. Grow in bright light; water moderately. A very handsome plant, highly recommended.

Spring: Keep soil evenly moist. Sun.
Summer: Provide ample moisture. Bright light.
Fall: Keep soil evenly moist. Bright light.

MUEHLENBECKIA COMPLEXA

wire plant

Here is a small plant that rarely grows more than a few inches and has round leaves; effective for basket growing. It grows rapidly into a tight mat of foliage and is quite unusual. It is a sun lover and resents overwatering. Keep the soil just barely moist.

All Year: Follow winter schedule.

MURRAEA EXOTICA

orange jasmine

An evergreen shrub that grows to about 36 inches and bears flowers that have an orange fragrance. The flowers are white and they are followed by red berries; a charming plant in bloom or out. Give sun and grow somewhat dry.

Spring: Keep evenly moist. Sun.
Summer: Provide ample water. Bright light.
Fall: Keep evenly moist. Sun.

MURRAEA PANICULATA

Often called satin wood, this plant grows slowly to 20 inches. The flowers are highly scented. Give it sun and grow somewhat dry.

Spring: Keep evenly moist. Sun.
Summer: Provide ample water. Bright light.
Fall: Keep evenly moist. Sun.

NARCISSUS TAZETTA

paper white narcissus

This is the fragrant narcissus that many people grow at Christmas time. While it is only good for the season, the scented white flowers are desirable additions in the home. Start five or six bulbs to a shallow pan of gravel; allow the tips of the bulbs to protrude slightly above the gravel line. Set in a shady place until growth starts. At that time move to a warm bright window and enjoy the lovely flowers.

See Chapter 7 for more information.

NEOMARICA GRACILIS

apostle plant

This dependable fragrant winter-flowering plant grows to about 30 inches. It has straplike foliage and lovely blue and white flowers. Give it full sun and plenty of water. After it blooms, rest the plant for about a month with scant waterings and then start it over again in fresh soil.

See Chapter 7 for more information.

NEOMARICA NORTHIANA

This plant is similar to *N. gracilis;* the difference is that the flowers are violet and white. Treat in the same manner.

See Chapter 7 for more information.

Medinilla magnifica

Muehlenbeckia complexa

Murraea exotica

Murraea paniculata

Narcissus tazetta

Neomarica gracilis

Neomarica northiana

NEPHROLEPIS 'FLUFFY RUFFLES'

A lovely 30-inch fern that lives up to its name; it requires bright or moderate light and evenly moist soil. Avoid getting water on the fronds.

Spring: Increase moisture somewhat. Bright light.
Summer: Provide ample moisture. Moderate light.
Fall: Keep soil evenly moist. Bright light.

NIDULARIUM FULGENS

Here is a pretty 24-inch rosette bromeliad with yellow-green foliage spotted dark green; the tiny white-to-pink flowers are in dense clusters. It is an excellent plant for moderate or low light locations. Keep the "vase" filled with water, the potting medium just barely moist. Pot in equal parts fine-grade fir bark and soil. Good under artificial light.

Spring: Increase waterings somewhat. Moderate light.
Summer: Provide ample moisture. Low light.
Fall: Keep soil evenly moist. Moderate light.

ODONTOGLOSSUM GRANDE   tiger orchid

With 12-inch leaves and long sprays of yellow and brown flowers in early spring, the tiger orchid is a popular and dependable plant. The flowers stay fresh for about a month, one flower opening as another fades. Give the plant plenty of sunlight and water except for a four-week rest before and then again after flowering. Grow in medium-grade fir bark.

Spring: Dry out to encourage flower buds. Sun.
Summer: Keep evenly moist. Bright light.
Fall: Keep evenly moist. Bright light.

ODONTOGLOSSUM PULCHELLUM

This small-leaved orchid has fragrant white flowers. Its display is not as abundant as the tiger orchid, but it is easy to grow and only needs coolness (60° F). Grow in bright light and provide moderate moisture.

Spring: Keep evenly moist. Bright light.
Summer: Keep evenly moist. No sun.
Fall: Increase moisture somewhat. Bright light.

ONCIDIUM AMPLIATUM   turtle orchid

With leathery leaves and 1-inch brown and yellow flowers in late winter, this 28-inch orchid deserves a spot at any bright window. Provide good air circulation and be sure the potting medium is moist. Pot in large-grade fir bark.

Spring: Dry out to encourage flower buds. Sun.
Summer: Keep evenly moist. Bright light.
Fall: Increase moisture somewhat. Bright light.

OXALIS CERNUA

This small oxalis bears cloverlike leaves and handsome yellow flowers in winter. It is hardly spectacular but it is a very handsome addition to the winter garden. Grow it in sun with plenty of water all year; it almost takes care of itself. Good in terrariums.

All Year: Follow winter schedule.

OXALIS RUBRA

This red oxalis bears its flowers in winter. Like all plants in this group, it is relatively easy to grow indoors with plenty of water and sunlight. Good in terrariums.

All Year: Follow winter schedule.

Nephrolepis 'Fluffy Ruffles'

Nidularium fulgens

Odontoglossum grande

Odontoglossum pulchellum

Oncidium ampliatum

Oxalis cernua

Oxalis rubra

PAPHIOPEDILUM FAIRIEANUM
ladyslipper orchid

With soft green leaves, this lovely 20-inch orchid bears 1-inch purple flowers in winter. It needs a cool (60° F) temperature and bright or moderate light. Keep the soil moderately moist. Pot in equal parts soil and fine-grade fir bark.

Spring: Keep evenly moist. Bright light.
Summer: Keep evenly moist. Bright light.
Fall: Keep evenly moist. Bright light.

PAPHIOPEDILUM SPICERIANUM
ladyslipper orchid

With 2-inch pale-green leaves and purple and white flowers in winter, this cool-growing orchid is a lovely addition to the indoor greenery during winter. It needs low or moderate light and an evenly moist growing medium. Pot in medium-grade fir bark.

Spring: Keep evenly moist. Bright light.
Summer: Keep evenly moist. Moderate light.
Fall: Keep evenly moist. Bright light.

PELLAEA ROTUNDIFOLIA
button fern

Low and spreading, with small dark-green leaves, this 14-inch plant is lovely for basket growing. It makes a handsome house plant but does need good drainage. Grow it in bright light; keep soil moist but avoid overwatering.

Spring: Keep evenly moist. Bright light.
Summer: Keep evenly moist. Bright light.
Fall: Dry out between waterings. Low light.

PELLAEA VIRIDIS

With large green leaflets and growing to about 24 inches, this is a climber. It's an unusual plant, hard to find, but adds nice green color to the winter room. Grow it in bright light and allow the soil to dry out between waterings.

Spring: Keep soil evenly moist. Bright light.
Summer: Keep soil evenly moist. Low light.
Fall: Dry out between waterings. Bright light.

PHILODENDRON RADIATUM

Growing to 40 inches, this vining philodendron has dark-green lobed leaves; handsome. Give the plant low or moderate light; keep soil moist.

Spring: Keep soil evenly moist. Moderate light.
Summer: Provide ample water. Moderate light.
Fall: Dry out between waterings. Moderate light.

PHILODENDRON SODIROI

A vining philodendron to about 40 inches, this plant bears lovely heart-shaped leaves and makes a spectacular room accent. It grows in moderate or low light and needs only even moisture.

Spring: Keep evenly moist. Bright light.
Summer: Increase moisture. Bright light.
Fall: Dry out between waterings. Bright light.

PITTOSPORUM TOBIRA

With thick leathery green leaves, this decorative evergreen grows to 48 inches. It likes slightly acid soil; grow in moderate or low light and keep the soil on the dry side. Pittosporum makes a lovely tub plant.

Spring: Increase moisture somewhat. Bright light.
Summer: Keep soil evenly moist. Moderate light.
Fall: Keep soil evenly moist. Moderate light.

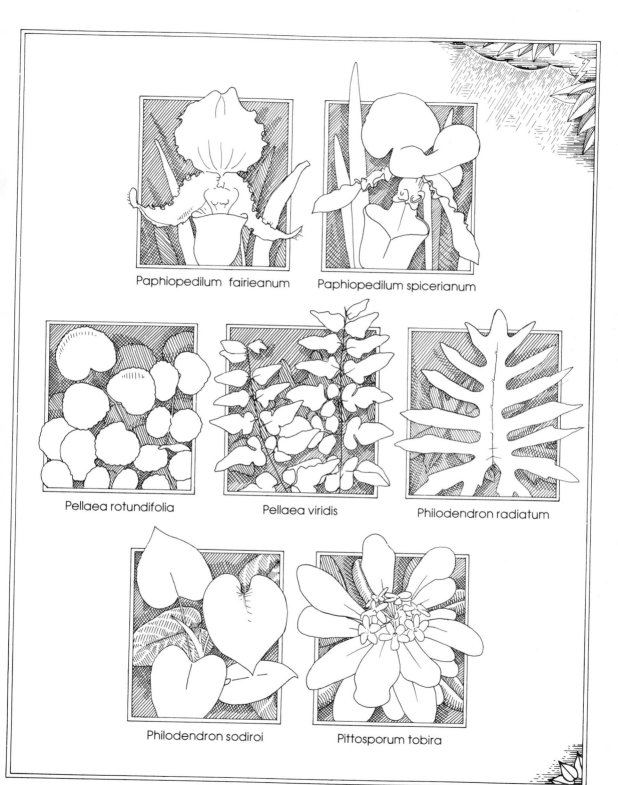

Paphiopedilum fairieanum

Paphiopedilum spicerianum

Pellaea rotundifolia

Pellaea viridis

Philodendron radiatum

Philodendron sodiroi

Pittosporum tobira

PITTOSPORUM VARIEGATUM
This is a variegated form of *P. tobira* and is treated in the same manner.

PLATYCERIUM BIFURCATUM   staghorn fern
An unusual fern with forked fronds, growing to 36 inches, this plant is best grown on an osmunda slab or piece of wood. The staghorn fern needs plenty of water; soak plant in a bucket. Bright light is fine.

Spring: Keep evenly moist. Bright light.
Summer: Provide ample water. Bright light.
Fall: Keep evenly moist. Bright light.

PODOCARPUS MACROPHYLLA   Southern yew
An erect branching plant to about 40 inches with waxy black and green leaves, this is a fine tub plant for rooms. It will tolerate low light; let soil dry out between waterings.

Spring: Increase moisture. Bright light.
Summer: Keep evenly moist. Bright light.
Fall: Dry out between waterings. Bright light.

PODOCARPUS NAGI
With spreading shiny green foliage and growing to about 40 inches, this lovely treelike plant is handsome indoors. Grow it in low or bright light and allow the soil to dry out between waterings.

Spring: Keep evenly moist. Bright light.
Summer: Keep evenly moist. Bright light.
Fall: Dry out between waterings. Sun.

REINWARDTIA INDICA   yellow flax
This 40-inch outdoor plant sometimes does well indoors and is valued for its yellow flowers. The plant needs coolness (60° F) and a bright location; keep soil barely moist.

Spring: Keep soil evenly moist. Bright light.
Summer: Keep soil evenly moist. Bright light.
Fall: Dry out between waterings. Bright light.

SCHEFFLERA ACTINOPHYLLA   umbrella tree
A very popular plant, fast-growing to 60 inches or more, with large decorative fronds and flowers in panicles. Give bright light and keep the soil just barely moist. Good wherever a large plant is needed.

Spring: Keep evenly moist. Bright light.
Summer: Dry out between waterings. Bright light.
Fall: Dry out between waterings. Bright light.

SOLANUM PSEUDO CAPSICUM   Jerusalem cherry
A favorite Christmas gift plant growing to 24 inches, this has white flowers and red fruit in winter. It is decorative for the window and easy to grow. It needs bright light; keep the soil barely moist. Grow cool, about 50° F, with little moisture during the winter months. If you want to hold it over from year to year, set the plant out in the garden in late spring and prune back to about 10 inches.

Pittosporum variegatum

Platycerium bifurcatum

Podocarpus macrophylla

Podocarpus nagi

Reinwardtia indica

Schefflera actinophylla

Solanum pseudo capsicum

SPARMANNIA AFRICANA
indoor linden

An evergreen plant growing to about 40 inches, with pale hairy leaves and charming white flowers in the dead of winter. It is an excellent window plant that will need some bright light and plenty of water all year. Because it grows so quickly, prune it occasionally to keep it within bounds.

Spring: Keep evenly moist. Bright light.
Summer: Keep evenly moist. Bright light.
Fall: Dry out between waterings. Sun.

SPATHIPHYLLUM CLEVELANDII

Growing to 20 inches, with long leaves and white flowers that appear in winter, this plant is excellent for indoor decoration. Give it moderate or low light and keep the soil evenly moist. Good under artificial light.

Spring: Keep soil evenly moist. Moderate light.
Summer: Keep soil evenly moist. Low light.
Fall: Dry out between waterings. Moderate light.

SPATHIPHYLLUM FLORIBUNDUM

This is a dwarf, growing to about 12 inches, with green leaves and lovely white flowers in winter. It will need a bright location; allow soil to dry out between waterings. A charming small plant, fine for artificial light gardens.

Spring: Keep soil evenly moist. Bright light.
Summer: Provide ample water. Bright light.
Fall: Dry out between waterings. Bright light.

THUNBERGIA ALATA
black-eyed Susan

An outdoor plant, this 40-inch vine can also grow indoors. It needs full sun and high heat. Keep the soil evenly moist except in winter, when plants can be almost dry. Train the black-eyed Susan to a pot trellis.

Spring: Keep soil evenly moist. Sun.
Summer: Flood soil with water. Sun.
Fall: Keep soil evenly moist. Sun.

TILLANDSIA CYANEA

This large tillandsia, growing to about 40 inches, with grassy foliage, bears an erect stem with unusual purple flowers. The plant grows best in moderate or low light; keep it evenly moist. Not easy to bring to bloom.

Spring: Follow winter schedule.
Summer: Increase waterings. Bright light.
Fall: Dry out between waterings. Moderate light.

TILLANDSIA IONANTHA

This small tufted bromeliad grows only 4 to 6 inches. At bloom time, in the middle of winter, the center of the plant turns fiery red; unusual and very pretty. *T. ionantha* needs little more than constant moisture and bright sun.

All Year: Follow winter schedule.

XANTHOSOMA LINDENII

With green and white leaves and growing to about 36 inches, this is a jungle plant known for its exquisite foliage. It needs bright light and an evenly moist soil along with high humidity, at least 50 percent. It may be difficult to accommodate this plant in most homes, but it is an exotic beauty.

Spring: Follow winter schedule.
Summer: Increase waterings. Bright light.
Fall: Dry out between waterings. Bright light.

ZYGOCACTUS TRUNCATUS
Christmas cactus

This well-known cactus grows to about 30 inches in diameter and has a striking display of red or pink flowers in December.
See Chapter 11 for yearly care schedule.

Sparmannia africana

Spathiphyllum clevelandii

Spathiphyllum floribundum

Thunbergia alata

Tillandsia cyanea

Tillandsia ionantha

Xanthosoma lindenii

Zygocactus truncatus

APPENDIX

COMMON NAME – BOTANICAL NAME REFERENCE

Common Name	Botanical Name	Season
African violet	Saintpaulia	Fall
Aluminum plant	*Pilea cadierii*	Summer
Amaryllis	Hippeastrum	Summer
Amazon lily	*Eucharis grandiflora*	Spring
Angel-wing begonia	*Begonia coccinea*	Spring
Apostle plant	*Neomarica gracilis*	Winter
Arrowhead plant	*Syngonium podophyllum*	Summer
Australian bracken	*Pteris tremula*	Fall
Ball cactus	*Notocactus ottonis*	Spring
Bamboo palm	*Chamaedorea erumpens*	Fall
Banana plant	*Musa velutina*	Spring
Beaver-tail cactus	*Opuntia basilaris*	Fall
Beefsteak begonia	*Begonia erythrophylla*	Fall
Bird-of-paradise	*Strelitzia reginae*	Fall
Bird's nest fern	*Asplenium nidus*	Spring
Black-eyed Susan	*Thunbergia alata*	Winter
Blood lily	*Haemanthus katherinae*	Spring
Blood lily	*Haemanthus multiflorus*	Spring
Blue sage	*Eranthemum nervosum*	Fall
Boston fern	*Nephrolepis Bostoniense*	Spring
Brazilian edelweiss	*Rechsteineria leucotricha*	Summer
Bunny-ear cactus	*Opuntia microdasys*	Fall
Burro's tail	*Sedum morganianum*	Summer
Buttercup orchid	*Dendrobium aggregatum*	Spring
Button fern	*Pellaea rotundifolia*	Winter
Calico flower	*Aristolochia elegans*	Spring
Calla lily	*Zantedeschia aethiopica*	Summer
Cape jasmine	*Gardenia jasminoides*	Summer
Carnival orchid	*Ascocentrum ampullaceum*	Spring
Castor bean begonia	*Begonia ricinifolia*	Spring
Century plant	*Agave victoriae reginae*	Winter
Chain orchid	*Lockhartia oerstedii*	Summer
Chenille plant	*Acalypha hispida*	Spring
Chinese evergreen	*Aglaonema commutatum*	Winter
Chinese evergreen	*Aglaonema modestum*	Fall
Chinese fan palm	*Livistona chinensis*	Fall
Christmas begonia	*Begonia cheimantha*	Winter
Christmas bromeliad	*Aechmea racinae*	Winter
Christmas cactus	*Zygocactus truncatus*	Winter
Cinnamon orchid	*Lycaste aromatica*	Spring
Climbing fern	*Lygodium japonicum*	Winter
Club moss	*Selaginella kraussiana*	Fall
Coffee plant	*Coffea arabica*	Winter

Common Name	Botanical Name	Season
Coralberry	*Ardisia crenata*	Winter
Coral plant	*Rusellia equisetiformis*	Summer
Corn plant	*Dracaena fragrans*	Winter
Cow's-horn orchid	*Stanhopea oculata*	Summer
Croton	*Codiaeum variegatum pictum*	Summer
Crown cactus	*Rebutia kupperiana*	Fall
Crown-of-thorns	*Euphorbia splendens*	Winter
Cup-and-saucer vine	*Cobea scandens*	Summer
Cup-of-gold	*Solandra longiflora*	Fall
Date palm	*Phoenix roebelenii*	Spring
Dragon plant	*Dracaena marginata*	Winter
Dumbcane	*Dieffenbachia amoena*	Spring
Dwarf orange	*Citrus taitensis*	Spring
Egyptian star flower	*Pentas lanceolata*	Fall
Elephant-ears	*Colocasia esculenta*	Winter
Emerald fern	*Asparagus sprengeri*	Winter
Eyelash begonia	*Begonia boweri*	Winter
False aralia	*Dizygotheca elegantissima*	Fall
Fan palm	*Chrysalidocarpus lutescens*	Winter
Fiddleleaf fig	*Ficus lyrata*	Spring
Fiddleleaf philodendron	*Philodendron panduraeforme*	Summer
Fingernail plant	*Neoregelia carolinae*	Fall
Fishtail palm	*Caryota mitis*	Fall
Flame-of-the-woods	*Ixora chinensis*	Spring
Flamingo flower	*Anthurium scherzerianum*	Winter
Flaming sword	*Vriesea splendens*	Summer
Flowering maple	*Abutilon hybridum*	Spring
Flowering onion	*Allium neapolitanum*	Winter
Fragrant daphne	*Daphne odora*	Winter
Geranium	Pelargonium	Spring
German violet	*Exacum affine*	Fall
Ginger lily	*Hedychium coronarium*	Fall
Glory bower	*Clerodendrum thomsoniae*	Summer
Glory bush	*Tibouchina semidecandra*	Fall
Glory lily	*Gloriosa rothschildiana*	Summer
Gold dust tree	*Aucuba japonica goldieana*	Winter
Golden barrel	*Echinocactus grusoni*	Summer
Golden calla	*Zantedeschia elliottiana*	Summer
Grape ivy	*Cissus rhombifolia*	Spring
Grape orchid	*Dendrobium densiflorum*	Spring
Grecian urn plant	*Acanthus montanus*	Summer
Hardy amaryllis	*Lycoris radiata*	Winter
Holly fern	*Cyrtomium falcatum*	Fall
Honeybells	*Mahernia verticillata*	Fall
Indoor linden	*Sparmannia africana*	Winter
Indoor oak	*Nicodemia diversifolia*	Fall
Iron cross begonia	*Begonia masoniana*	Spring

Common Name	Botanical Name	Season
Ivy arum	*Scindapsus aureus*	Summer
Jacobean lily	*Sprekelia formosissima*	Spring
Jade tree	*Crassula argentea*	Fall
Jerusalem cherry	*Solanum pseudo capsicum*	Winter
Kafir lily	*Clivia miniata*	Spring
Kangaroo thorn	*Acacia armata*	Spring
Kangaroo vine	*Cissus antarctica*	Spring
Kentia palm	*Howea balmoreana*	Fall
Lace aloe	*Aloe aristata*	Winter
Lace cactus	*Echinocereus reichenbachii*	Summer
Lady-of-the-night	*Brassavola nodosa*	Fall
Lady palm	*Rhapis excelsa*	Spring
Lady's eardrops	Fuchsia	Summer
Ladyslipper orchid	*Paphiopedilum fairieanum*	Winter
Ladyslipper orchid	*Paphiopedilum spicerianum*	Winter
Leadwort	*Plumbago capensis*	Summer
Lemon vine	*Pereskia aculeata*	Fall
Lily-of-the-Nile	*Agapanthus africanus*	Summer
Lipstick vine	*Aeschynanthus speciosus*	Summer
Love plant	*Medinilla magnifica*	Winter
Madagascar jasmine	*Stephanotis floribunda*	Spring
Maidenhair fern	*Adiantum tenerum*	Spring
Maple leaf begonia	*Begonia dregei*	Spring
Mexican firecracker	*Manettia inflata*	Winter
Mexican foxglove	*Allophytum mexicanum*	Fall
Mexican love vine	*Dipladenia amoena*	Summer
Ming tree	*Polyscias balfouriana*	Fall
Miniature bamboo	*Bambusa nana*	Spring
Miniature bamboo	*Sasa pygmaea*	Spring
Miniature pineapple	*Ananas nana*	Summer
Miniature rose	*Rosa chinensis minima*	Spring
Miniature wax plant	*Hoya bella*	Summer
Mistletoe fig	*Ficus diversifolia*	Spring
Moses-in-a-boat	*Rhoeo discolor*	Spring
Natal plum	*Carissa grandiflora*	Winter
Norfolk Island pine	*Araucaria excelsa*	Winter
Old man cactus	*Cephalocereus palmeri*	Fall
Oleander	*Nerium oleander*	Summer
Orange jasmine	*Murraea exotica*	Winter
Orchid cactus	Epiphyllum	Summer
Palm leaf begonia	*Begonia luxurians*	Spring
Panda plant	*Kalanchoe tomentosa*	Winter
Paper flower	Bougainvillea	Spring
Paper white narcissus	*Narcissus tazetta*	Winter
Parlor palm	*Chamaedorea elegans*	Fall
Parrot flower	*Heliconia psitticorum*	Spring
Passion flower	*Passiflora caerulea*	Spring

Common Name	Botanical Name	Season
Passion flower	*Passiflora trifasciata*	Spring
Peacock plant	*Kaempfera roscoeana*	Summer
Piggyback plant	*Tolmiea menziesii*	Summer
Pincushion cactus	*Mammillaria bocasana*	Summer
Pincushion cactus	*Mammillaria hahniana*	Winter
Pineapple lily	*Eucomis punctata*	Summer
Pineapple plant	*Ananas cosmosus*	Summer
Pink calla	*Zantedeschia rehmanni*	Summer
Pocketbook plant	Calceolaria	Spring
Poet's jasmine	*Jasminium officinale grandiflora*	Fall
Poinsettia	*Euphorbia pulcherrima*	Winter
Polka-dot plant	*Hypoestes sanguinolenta*	Summer
Pomegranate	*Punica granatum*	Fall
Pony Tail	*Beaucarnia recurvata*	Summer
Prayer plant	*Maranta leuconeura massangeana*	Fall
Purple velvet plant	*Gynura aurantiaca*	Winter
Pussy-ears	*Cyanotis somaliense*	Spring
Queen's tears	*Billbergia nutans*	Winter
Queen's wreath	*Petrea volubilis*	Spring
Rabbit's foot fern	*Davallia bullata mariesii*	Spring
Rainbow flower	*Achimenes grandiflora*	Summer
Rainbow flower	*Achimenes longiflora*	Summer
Red-hot-poker plant	*Guzmania monostachia*	Spring
Red pepper plant	*Capsicum annuum*	Fall
Rose-of-China	*Hibiscus rosa-sinensis*	Fall
Rouge plant	*Rivina humilis*	Fall
Rubber plant	*Ficus elastica*	Spring
Sago palm	*Cycas revoluta*	Fall
Scarborough lily	*Vallota speciosa*	Spring
Screw pine	*Pandanus veitchii*	Summer
Shooting star	Cyclamen	Winter
Shrimp plant	*Beloperone guttata*	Summer
Silk oak	*Grevillea robusta*	Winter
Silver urn plant	*Aechmea fasciata*	Fall
Snake plant	*Sansevieria trifasciata*	Summer
Society garlic	*Tulbaghia fragrans*	Summer
Southern yew	*Podocarpus macrophylla*	Winter
Spanish shawl	*Schizocentron elegans*	Summer
Spider orchid	*Ansellia gigantea*	Summer
Spider plant	*Chlorophytum elatum*	Winter
Spiral ginger	*Costus igneus*	Summer
Spleenwort fern	*Asplenium viviparum*	Spring
Staghorn fern	*Platycerium bifurcatum*	Winter
Star begonia	*Begonia heracifolia*	Winter
Star cactus	*Astrophytum asterias*	Fall
Star of Bethlehem	*Campanula isophyllus*	Fall
String-of-hearts	*Ceropegia woodii*	Winter

Common Name	Botanical Name	Season
Swedish ivy	*Plectranthus australis*	Summer
Swedish ivy	*Plectranthus oertendahii*	Summer
Sweet flag	*Acorus gramineus*	Winter
Sweet olive	*Osmanthus fragrans*	Fall
Swiss cheese plant	*Monstera deliciosa*	Fall
Table fern	*Pteris cretica* 'Wilsonii'	Fall
Tapestry plant	*Cissus discolor*	Spring
Temple bells	*Smithiantha cinnabarina*	Fall
Tiger orchid	*Odontoglossum grande*	Winter
Ti-plant	*Cordyline terminalis*	Fall
Turtle orchid	*Oncidium ampliatum*	Winter
Umbrella tree	*Schefflera actinophylla*	Winter
Wandering Jew	*Tradescantia blossfeldiana*	Summer
Wandering Jew	*Tradescantia flumensis*	Summer
Wandering Jew	*Zebrina pendula*	Summer
Wax plant	*Hoya carnosa*	Summer
Weeping fig	*Ficus benjamina*	Spring
Wire plant	*Muehlenbeckia complexa*	Winter
Wood sorrel	*Oxalis hirta*	Fall
Yellow flax	*Reinwardtia indica*	Winter
Zebra plant	*Aphelandra chamaissiona*	Summer

INDEX TO PLANTS

213